Electronic music production

Complete electronic music studio in London

Electronic music production

ALAN DOUGLAS

Senior Member IEEE
Associate, Incorporated
Society of Organ Builders

TAB BOOKS
Blue Ridge Summit, Pa. 17214

FIRST EDITION

FIRST PRINTING—APRIL 1974
SECOND PRINTING—JANUARY 1976

Copyright © Alan Douglas 1973

Printed in the United States
of America

Hardbound Edition: International Standard Book No. 0-8306-4718-X

Paperbound Edition: International Standard Book No. 0-8306-3718-4

Library of Congress Card Number: 74-75216

Also published in England by Pitman Publishing

Preface

"Music was forced to shape for itself the material on which it works. Painting and sculpture find the fundamental character of their materials, form and colour, in nature itself, which they strive to imitate. Poetry finds its material ready formed in the words of language. Music alone finds an infinitely rich but totally shapeless plastic material in the tones of musical instruments. There is a greater and more absolute freedom in the use of material for music than for any of the other arts; but certainly it is more difficult to make a proper use of absolute freedom."

So wrote von Helmholtz in 1880. What remarkable insight and how very true.

The many forms through which music has passed through the ages indicate that there is a time and place for everything. When Wagner's "Tannhaüser" was first performed, an eminent critic wrote: "It seems to me that a man who will not only write such a thing, but actually have it printed, has little call for an artistic career." Today the public is more tolerant, and instead of being bound by convention is indeed very forward looking. Thus we can welcome the introduction of electronic music as a real entity, an art in its own right; and if Helmholtz's words are carefully studied, and we do not try to run before we can walk, this music will become as firmly established as is Tannhaüser. This is of course the danger; the whole art is so new, and everything associated with it is so fluid, that there is temptation to use the method just for the sake of the tremendous potential of a new creative medium.

Preface

It will take time and experience for musicians to adjust their thinking in terms of the abstract, in terms of the basic ingredients of the sound instead of the finished sound itself.

It would not be possible to write a book of this kind without drawing on the experience of the pioneers of this art; and on the ingenuity of the circuit designers, who for the first time have become as important as the composers themselves. Grateful acknowledgement is therefore made to the following individuals and companies for the use of material first described by them, and for the use of certain diagrams or circuits.

Philips Technical Review, Vol. 19, No. 6, 1957.

Technische Hausmitteilungen NWDR, 8–15, 1954.

Journal of the Audio Engineering Society, New York, N.Y.

Music, Physics and Engineering, Dover Publications Inc, New York, N.Y., U.S.A.

Dr. Hugh le Caine, National Research Council, Ottawa, Canada.

Dr. Harry Olson, RCA Laboratories, Princeton, N.J., U.S.A.

Professor Milton Babbitt, Columbia University, New York, N.Y., U.S.A.

Max Matthews, Bell Laboratories, Murray Hill, N.J., U.S.A.

Peter Zinovieff, Electronic Music Studios, London.

Daphne Oram, Tower Folly, Fairseat, Wrotham, Kent.

Robert A. Moog, Moog Laboratories, Trumansburg, N.Y., U.S.A.

Gustav Ciamaga, University of Toronto, Toronto, Canada.

Further references will be found in the bibliography at the end of the text.

It is hoped that this book will serve as an introduction to some of the many facets of this new medium, and perhaps to stimulate thought for further developments.

ALAN DOUGLAS

Contents

Introduction

Music has been produced in all countries and all civilizations since time immemorial. Elementary and vocal in origin, as instruments began to be developed so the complexity of the music increased. The Western world developed more rapidly than the East, and we find the means for composing and interpreting written music advancing at roughly the same rates. As composers required new tone colours and effects, these were provided by improved instruments.

This process continued into the 19th century, when physics could no longer provide extensions to the power, pitch or manipulative characteristics of conventional musical instruments. There were limits to these characteristics and composers had no alternative but to write within these limits. Convention was very strong and communication of musical ideas was only possible by concerts or by performances in the home. The ability to bring new music to the people was limited by these conditions.

With the advent of broadcasting the listening public increased enormously in numbers and, with the introduction of electrical gramophone recording, music in all forms could be studied and appreciated at any time or in any place. Nonetheless, conservatism in musical form or the geometry of composition was limited to well-known classical types of structure. The public was not ready for departures from existing practice.

Many early experimenters in all forms of art—or science—

were frustrated by the lack of means to interpret their ideas. Many of us can recall the days when even to receive a broadcast called for some manipulative skill with sometimes uncertain results. But advances in electronics since the last war have now provided powerful and stable tools with which to overcome many of the limitations of conventional instruments and to provide new ones. Art reflects the age in which it was born, but today the means are there as well.

So now we must ask ourselves, why do we want these new devices, and what are we going to do with them?

We define electronic music as the production of waveforms by electrical oscillations, that is, the source is itself inaudible and is not in the form of air pressure waves, to which alone the ear can respond.

The oscillations, however generated, are then processed by electronic circuitry into desired forms which can be converted into audible sounds through the medium of electro-acoustic transducers, commonly one or more loudspeakers. So we can see that the distinguishing features of all electrically generated sounds are that the source itself cannot be heard; and that the initial oscillations or vibrations are of small amplitude, and therefore have little energy.

Since waveforms of a regularly-recurring and cyclic pattern constitute music, whilst those of irregular, transient or spasmodic form constitute noise, it is easy to see that effects ranging from a pure tone (like a tuning fork) to bursts of noise (like a machine gun) can be generated by suitable electrical means, because today we are able to produce simultaneously any kind of oscillation of any frequency and as many as we need. Then, because of the universal use of the tape recorder, any form of subsequent processing, re-recording and storage is possible.

Music, of any nature whatsoever, derives from a combination of three parameters only: pitch, intensity and duration. These can be broken down in a more precise and analytical way. To form a complete musical sound as at present understood requires a pitch or frequency, a rate at which the sound starts, a period over which it is maintained, and a rate at which it decays and disappears. Then there will be added harmonics, overtones or partials, probably noise due to the method of generation, and of course a loudness or intensity level (not necessarily fixed). Additionally, there may be second-order effects such as reverberation and vibrato.

It is evident that a parameter such as frequency can be exactly specified, but any factor depending on a time scale is less precise. For this reason, conventional notation can only delineate pitch or frequency with any real accuracy, the absolute value of a written note being related to the absolute value of other notes in a rather loose way. The envelope characteristics are even more difficult to specify. This expression embraces the whole period of time for which the note is sounding, and includes the starting time, the holding time and the decay time. Since these attributes are also bound up with the intensity or loudness, it can be seen that envelope control is both complex and important. In all these basic respects, electronic music generators can prove much superior and infinitely more flexible than any conventional music generator.

We will see in Chapter I that the introduction of harmonics to colour the pitch note is almost entirely dependent on the physical properties of the instrument, and of course this is the exact opposite of electronically produced sound where there is no timbre until specified and inserted by the operator, with the exception of elementary apparatus for experimental purposes.

Electronic music falls into two classes: tone production and forming, and composing. Neither of these fields suffer from any of the limitations imposed on or by conventional musical instruments. Yet, because of the long established status of the orchestral instrument, we should see how the sounds derived from such instruments are produced, and what shortcomings they may have. For it is one of the aims of electronic music to overcome these deficiencies, some of which are explained presently.

It might be thought that a prime aim of electronic music was to displace the human performer entirely in the course of time. Of course, there are schools of thought with this in mind; nevertheless, it seems highly improbable that this will ever come about, and it is much more likely that electronic music and composition per se will provide another art form, having its own language, performers and devotees.

Let us then look at some of the limitations of conventional physical instruments. Ever since the introduction of temperament, or any form of relating the various notes of the scale, many instruments have been designed with valves or keys producing fixed intervals between adjacent notes. It is clear that such a construction is an essential part of a piano or organ, and it is employed in all woodwind and brass instruments except the trombone. Music must conform with these intervals to be playable at all. But this construction confers one very great advantage—it is unfailingly repetitive, that is, pressing the same key will always produce the same note. This enables music to be written with accuracy.

At the same time, we have the string family, which is characterized by having no fixed intervals; one can play a quarter tone, tenth tone, or any other fraction. This family, then, though capable of playing any pitch within its limits, must still conform to the fixed temperament of other instruments. It is evident at once that if other instruments could be made to play in any desired fraction of an interval (of the existing temperament), a vast number of new musical forms and patterns would become available.

Next, there is the question of power or loudness output from any individual instrument. Detailed information on this is given later on, but obviously there is a limit to the degree of vibration possible, whether it be a string or an air column. For more power one must therefore have more instruments. This at once leads to possible lack of accuracy in interpreting, and certainly differences in harmonic texture or timbre between individuals in a group.

Then consider the pitch range. This must be limited by the need for compactness and ease of manipulation, apart from the fact that the stimulating energy must be imparted by human means and the performer has limited stamina. Moreover, in nearly every conventional instrument, there are marked differences in both the power and quality of the extreme upper and lower notes, so that one cannot really exploit the full range of notes possible with equal effect. In any case, no one instrument can cover the whole compass of notes required for that quality of sound—the violin must give way to the viola, then the 'cello, then the bass viol to cover the possible range required by the composer for string tone. It would be very desirable to overcome these limitations and extend the composer's powers.

Let us then approach the question of noise and non-musical sounds accompanying the tone band. Virtually all orchestral instruments depend on resonant systems to develop the power required. It is well known that much more power is required to start a coupled system resonating than to maintain it in that condition, but it is not possible to reduce the energy by much once it has been applied. The excess power then appears as noise. This is very marked in bowed instruments, particularly where the tone band is widely separated from the noise band, as in the bass viol for example, or where the applied power must always be great to get the instrument to speak at all, as in the piccolo.

There are clicks from valves and noise from the impact of piano or xylophone hammers, and excessive wind noise from the organ. When a mute is used on a violin, the bowing noise may be almost as great as the tone engendered. We accept these imperfections because we have been brought up with them, but this is not to say it is a good thing.

No instrument depending on resonance can release its energy instantly, though it may start vibrating almost at once if enough force is applied; so there is a natural rate of attack and decay for all conventional instruments. If damping is applied to bring about a quicker cessation of the sound, then the shape of the decay curve is altered and the effect is often unreal. Many new musical effects are possible if there is control over the starting and stopping rates of a musical sound and this is possible by electronic means.

Lastly, the range of musical percussions is limited with physical instruments; there is a big gap here in the orchestral spectrum, easily filled electronically. The same applies to non-musical percussions, e.g., triangle, drums, wood blocks, cymbals, etc. The difficulty of getting a cymbal to ring continuously, for instance, is readily solved by synthetic means.

If we add the whole of these possible limitations together, coupled with the difficulty of manipulating many instruments (and even the uncertainty, as in the French horn), we shall see in this book that in addition to overcoming them by electronic means, we are able to vastly increase the power and pitch range; obtain crescendos and diminuendos impossible with conventional instruments; divide the scaling into an infinite number of parts; obtain any degree of glissando or sliding scale; form completely new tone colours; supply echo or reverberation to any required extent and vary this at any instant as may be needed; produce arpeggios or similar progressions at a greater rate than is possible by human agency; and certainly in some cases, make the technique of playing a particular instrument very much easier. In short, to open up a whole new world of possibilities to the composer who cares to take advantage of these methods. Already it is possible for the student to practice harmony or composition at home on headphones by electronic means, so causing no disturbance to others; and whilst some space is devoted in this book to composing by mechanical means, it is not thought possible ever to dispense with the human brain. Science can greatly aid the musician today, but science and art do not speak the same language and it would be disastrous if music became completely automated.

In the opinion of the author, it is a combination of the conventional and the unconventional which will extract the best from music in times to come; and this would appear to agree with future economic as well as artistic trends.

1 Properties of conventional musical instruments

Now we have said that one purpose of electronic music is to extend, by means of synthesis, the range and quality of established orchestral instruments. So it is as well to understand how the quality of tone associated with a particular instrument is produced. The construction, mechanism and materials used, as well as the method of playing or manipulation, all influence the final sound spectrum.

Synthesis of some instruments is difficult and confers no advantage over the physical instrument. But some have gross defects, extreme difficulty in playing, and an uneven frequency response. Firstly it is as well to remember that no known orchestral instrument maintains its fundamental pitch and the *same* retinue of harmonics for more than a second or so. Every change in loudness or in pitch is accompanied by a change in the harmonic structure. This is because of the delicacy in control exercised by the player, the net effect being to prevent monotony of tone and to heighten the aesthetic appeal. This statement must be related to the form and purpose of the music being played, as witness the differing interpretations of the same piece of music under different conductors, using the same instruments. Let us look briefly at how some of the principal families of tone are produced.

The oboe

This instrument consists of a small mouthpiece holding an exposed reed, which is immersed in the breath of the player. The reed is attached to the narrow end of a slightly conical tube. The reed is double or consists of one reed doubled back on itself, and is made from thin cane, as shown in Fig. 1. It can

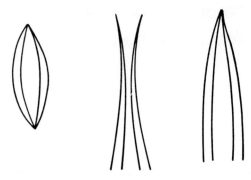

Fig 1   Oboe reed

vibrate both transversely and longitudinally. In the course of such vibrations, the small gap at the top end is alternately opened and closed, allowing pulses of air from the player's mouth to pass into the upper or narrow end of the tube which forms the body of the instrument. This latter controls the pitch note, the tones proper to the reed itself being much higher in pitch. Wood is used for the construction, and this is of great rigidity. When an air column is in a state of vibration in any constraining device such as a pipe or tube, should there be any tendency for the walls of the tube to be elastic, the intensity of any harmonic happening to have an antinode near to the point of flexure will be reduced in amplitude, since part of the energy of the wave will be used to deform the wall of the tube; the tone will sound duller and will lose carrying power.

The conical form of the tube permits of the full harmonic series of tones being developed, in spite of the fact that the tube is substantially closed at the upper end. This harmonic series is of course necessary properly to reinforce the characteristic tone of the reed, but the excitation of these various modes is governed by the so-called "formant" frequencies of the whole system. It is well known that each kind of vibration device has a band of frequencies which predominates no matter what fundamental or pitch note is being played. These fixed bands appear for every note within the compass of the instrument, and in Fig. 2 we can see some of the more common formant bands for

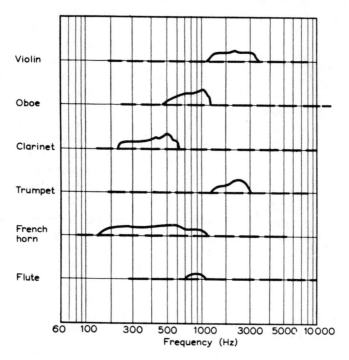

Fig 2   Formant bands of some conventional instruments

different instruments. These should be noted, since synthesis of many orchestral sounds involves the creation of formant bands by means of electrical resonant circuits. The materials of which the resonating tube is made are mainly responsible for the composition of a particular formant group, and certainly it is this which gives the shrill yet plaintive tone to the oboe, for, since all harmonics can be excited in the body, unless this were so the tone would be much smoother and rounder, there being no particular reason why one harmonic should be more prominent than another.

It might not seem very relevant to note the process by which a cone open at the base only can produce practically the full series of harmonics, that is, the equivalent of a parallel pipe open at both ends, but this gives an important clue as to why a change in geometry can alter the proportions, number and power of harmonics in instrument resonators. By combining a conical tube with a cylindrical parallel tube so that the major control is due to either one or the other form of tube; or by proportioning the fractions of each tube in an empirical way brought about by experiment, the harmonics proper to the vibrator or to the air column may be reinforced; or, it may be possible to force the air column to produce some series of partials which may not be strictly harmonic. It is this desirability of balancing one state against another state, over as wide a range of pitch and power as possible, which accounts for the fact that almost every orchestral wind instrument has a resonating tube combining, in part, the properties of a cone and a parallel cylinder.

Without deriving the full equations for the above conditions as applied to the oboe and taking R as the slant length of the cone, N_m as the frequency of the mth natural harmonic, λ_m as its wavelength and a as the speed of sound, we have

$$R = m\lambda_m/2 \qquad \text{or} \qquad N_m = ma/2R$$

giving almost the same fundamental and full harmonic series of tones as from a parallel pipe of the same length open at both

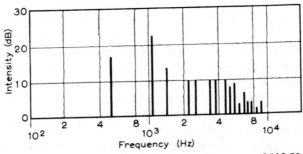

Fig 3   Spectrum of orchestral oboe at frequency of 523 Hz

ends. We might note in passing that the oboe is little affected by temperature, the percentage increase in frequency of the instrument for a rise of 10°F is only 0·31, about one half of that of other instruments. For this reason it is used as a pitch standard for tuning other orchestral instruments. Moreover, its penetrating quality of tone is readily heard above the sound of other instruments.

Finally, in Fig. 3 we show a characteristic harmonic analysis for $f = 523$ Hz. The comparatively weak fundamental will be noticed.

The clarinet

Although at first sight the oboe and clarinet appear very alike physically, the mechanism of tone production is quite different. The tube of the clarinet is cylindrical and the reed is of the single beating type, as in Fig. 4, which shows the reed open and

Fig 4   Clarinet reed, open and closed

closed. It is also made from cane but is much wider than the oboe reed. Whereas the oboe reed opens and closes more or less symmetrically with time, the reed of the clarinet tends to remain closed for a long time in any one cycle of operations, then opens rapidly to the full extent. The body is made from very hard wood and can also be made of metal; the tone is then harder and louder than that of a wooden one, as is to be expected from the reduced internal damping and the higher rate of transmission of sound waves in metal. Since the tube has parallel walls, plane waves are propagated, and hence the reed end of the tube is a node; only odd harmonics will be radiated, although there are small traces of even ones as well. The fundamental tone is about three times as powerful as the most significant formant tone. This is because the reed is broad, and the hollow-sounding nature of an odd harmonic system tends to be apparently more full and mellow than one in which all harmonics are engendered. Note, however, that whilst the oboe maintains its peculiar quality over the whole compass, the tone of the clarinet becomes harder in the upper register. A frequency spectrum of a typical clarinet is shown in Fig. 5.

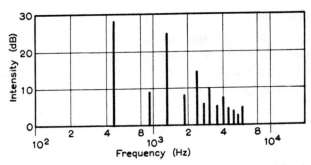

Fig 5   Spectrum of orchestral clarinet at frequency of 465 Hz

The trumpet

This is an instrument of the "labial" type, in which there is no actual reed, the lips of the player taking its place. It has the reputation of being the most brilliant of the brass instruments, but this is to some extent due to the pitch range, which is in a favourable position for stimulating the ear. The actual power output in fact is much less than that of the trombone. A high blowing pressure is required to force the air in the 6 ft long tube into resonance with the lips. Figure 6 shows the cupped mouthpiece having rings spun into the tube to form constrictions. The action of these is as follows.

When a jet of air issues from a circular orifice there is a tendency for it to curl up into vortex rings. These can be ranged into an orderly procession by making the issuing air strike an edge. In this case it is a circular edge. The distances between successive vortices then becomes equal to, or a sub-multiple of, the distance from the orifice of the jet to the circular edge facing it. The pitch of the note due to the vortices striking

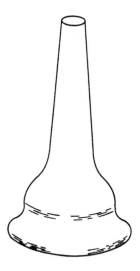

Fig 6   Mouthpiece of trumpet

the edge is related to the velocity of the jet and with the distance from orifice to edge. By making this last distance very small, we can get very high pitched notes. The formula for the normal production of these edge tones then becomes

$$\text{Pitch of edge tone} = \frac{\frac{1}{3}(\text{Velocity of issuing breath})}{\text{Distance from lips to mouthpiece flange}}$$

So to produce a high note the player should press the lips in towards the flange as well as increase the speed or pressure of his breath; and of course the tension on the lips must be increased as well.

The material of which the tube is made influences the tone; brass is common, silver produces a duller tone. In all cases the last foot or so rapidly expands into a flared mouth. A harmonic spectrum of a trumpet is given in Fig. 7. The sound is easily synthesized electrically with many variants.

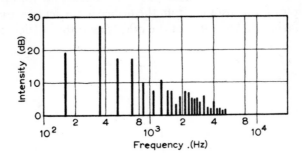

Fig 7   Spectrum of orchestral trumpet at frequency of 175 Hz

The flute

Sounds of this nature are the most commonly synthesized, for the obvious reason that they are very simple and very easily generated. But one must beware of this apparent simplicity, for indeed orchestral flute tone contains many harmonics with many shades of expression. The tone-producing elements consist of a circular orifice forming an edge tone generator, closely coupled to an adjustable resonating tube. The player blows, not into but across the circular mouth hole, so that his breath strikes the opposite edge. The more massive air column in the tube reinforces the harmonics proper to the particular pitch, and extinguishes any other overtones purely due to the edge tone though these can be clearly heard if one approaches the player closely. But the tone quality is quite different in the different octaves. This is because to extend the range, the blowing pressure is increased, so that the edge tone jumps up an octave, when the same note holes in the tube are used again; and yet again to complete the top octave. It is in this harmonic generation process that the quality of the sound becomes different, for the following reasons.

The small reduction in tube diameter near the mouth hole causes the pitch of the overtones to be slightly lowered, and the higher the pitch, the greater this effect. So that, since the second and third octaves are obtained from overtones of the fundamental by over-blowing, there will be a disproportionate rise in pitch as the frequency rises. There is a device in the air column to allow of fractional tuning of the resonator, but this does not bring the system completely into tune. The player may however do so by lip and breath manipulation at his discretion. And as the pitch of these notes is forced nearer to or further from the harmonic series of the tube, the quality of the sound changes in

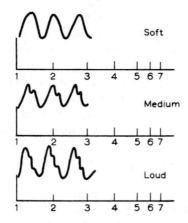

Fig 8   Analysis of flute tone

a way determined by the playing technique. Therefore, in Fig. 8 we show loud, medium and soft tones to show how the harmonic content varies with pitch and power. It is clear that true synthesis is very difficult.

Stringed instruments

With the exception of the trombone, wind instruments have fixed pitch intervals determined by the position of the holes or valves in the air column. However, by exceptional lip and fingering ability, skilled players can produce a glissando on certain of these instruments.

In the string family we find several very different features. In the first place, they are all capable of an infinite pitch series depending only on the ability of the performer; save that the lowest pitch is always fixed by the lowest natural frequency of the string in use and the dimensions of the body or resonator. Secondly, quite different kinds of tone quality can be obtained from each instrument, by bowing in different ways or by plucking the strings; by striking them and by using a mute. So there is enormous versatility in use, virtually unlimited, and for this reason it is difficult to specify a set of conditions which truly represent any vibratile state of the violin, violincello or bass viol.

It must be made clear that the purpose of the strings is to drive the body of the instrument, since by themselves they radiate no energy to the air; their small cross-section allows the air to flow round them unhindered, and no sound comes from them, certainly not for more than a few inches away. However, the strings are made from certain specified materials to regularize bowing technique and to impart enough energy to the body. This latter moves a large amount of free air and so transmits sufficient energy to be heard at a distance. The aim of the designer is to make the body act as a sounding board and not a resonator.

Without going into the theory of the system, it should be noted that the width of the bow may be comparable with the length of the string for many frequencies, which will not then sound; if the string is plucked with a sharp object, such as the finger nail, these frequencies will sound and the tone becomes harder and sharper. Many of these effects can be synthesized as we shall see later on. A typical spectrum of a violin sounding a quite steady note is given in Fig. 9. The functioning of the

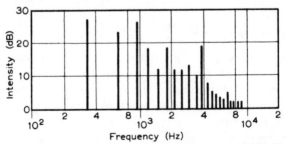

Fig 9   Spectrum of violin at frequency of 294 Hz

violincello and bass viol is quite similar, except that in the latter, the dimensions of the body do not often encourage the proper development of the very lowest notes, which sound weak.

It is noteworthy that a trained violinist will play in perfect pitch, so that during a violin solo with piano accompaniment it has been thought that the discrepancy in pitch is a fault in intonation; but in fact it is the piano which is wrong, as we shall see.

It is not necessary to go into the theory underlying the action of a stretched string, for those interested there are ample references at the end of this book. Suffice it to say that research on the properties of the viole family has occupied many investigators for a long time, but nothing of a practical nature which was not known to the violin makers of two hundred years ago appears to have come from this work.

The guitar may be bracketed with the violes, since it employs stretched strings. However, the strings are heavier and the body is larger for the pitch range. The strings also terminate on a flexible bridge, and the whole acoustic system is more yielding, so that a louder sound is produced and there is an appreciable delay in the cessation of the sound, as in Fig. 10. Of course,

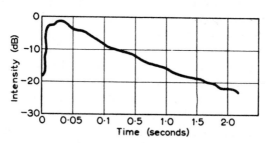

Fig 10   Decay curve of guitar

a bow is not used and it is usual to provide frets or bars positioned to indicate the position for stopping the strings for various notes. Today the electric guitar permits of a quite different tonal spectrum because the vibrations are picked up by magnetic means and the body has no influence on the tone quality. Since the pickups are very sensitive, the vibrations may continue much longer than with the acoustic instrument, where the energy soon falls below the level required to excite the sound-board.

The pipe organ

This is not a book on the organ, so we will only deal with some of the characteristics open to synthesis in a general way. The church or concert organ is based on the diapason, a pipe with a peculiar sound which is not a flute and not a string; there are literally thousands of different schools of diapason voicing. The pipes are usually of metal, and cover a range from very low notes of 16 Hz to extremely high ones, 8 kHz and above. The theatre organ rests on the tibia chorus, and this is a large flute often made of wood. It may also cover a very wide range of pitch. Other metal pipes produce string tones and pure flute tones. All these pipes function by a stream of air issuing from a slot in the pipe and vibrating a lip on the main tube, which, in starting to vibrate, quickly causes the air column in the tube to come into resonance, so generating a loud sound.

Most of these pipes are in octave relationship, that is, the different tonal effects are of 16, 8, 4 and 2 ft pitches; but a very important group of pipes is to be found in the mixtures and mutations. Because the larger and more powerful of the dia-pasons tend to be poor in harmonic development, additional ranks inject these missing harmonics and in fact allow of some control of the total number of harmonics present by adjusting the number of these extra ranks. We therefore find that pitches of 10.2/3, 5.1/3, 2.2/3, 1.3/5 and still more complex fractions may be present and these can be used to greatly heighten the value of the flue pipes constituting the main body of sound. The use of such fractional pitches will be examined when we look at electrical synthesis.

In addition to the pipes just mentioned, there are many imitating reed sounds, some conventional such as the oboe, trumpet or clarinet, some exclusive to the organ, such as the tuba, tromba and ophicleide. All of these function by having a vibrating metal reed in an enclosure which holds the reed firmly and at the same time prevents the sound of the actual reed from being heard. A resonating tube attached to the top of the reed assembly, or boot as it is called, emphasizes the proper pitch note of the pipe and reduces or eliminates the discordant harmonics which would otherwise be heard—as for example in the harmonium, where the reeds are not supplied with resonators and have a rather harsh sound as a consequence. By way of illustration, we show the spectrum of a vibrating reed alone, Fig. 11, and the same reed when attached to a tuned pipe, Fig. 12. The "filtering" action of the pipe is evident.

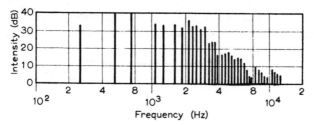

Fig 11   Spectrum of reed tongue alone at frequency of 262 Hz

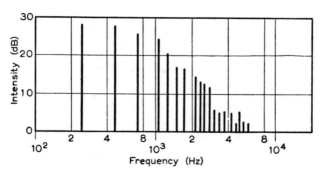

Fig 12   Spectrum of reed tongue plus resonating tube at frequency of 262 Hz

One aspect of the open metal pipe should be mentioned, as it is most difficult to synthesize. All pipes must be mounted, and of course there has to be a valve to admit wind when required. The geometry of this system greatly influences the rate and the manner in which the pipe speaks. If we consider a pipe standing on a wind chest, there will be static air in the foot of the pipe when at rest. This foot is only a support and takes no part in tone production, but it can hold a lot of air in a large pipe, and this must be driven out before the wind reaches the lip. Clearly any pipe has mass, which has to be set into vibration by a suddenly applied puff of wind. This cannot be instantaneous, and when the valve is first opened, the rush of wind causes a momentary false transient to appear, often audibly. As the wind continues to flow, the transient gradually becomes weaker as the lip begins to vibrate. During the rise in amplitude of the vibrations of the pipe the apparent frequency of the vibration is neither that of the transient or that of the exciting force; it is a variable composite of the two which approaches the steady-state frequency as the transient disappears. Figure 13 shows how

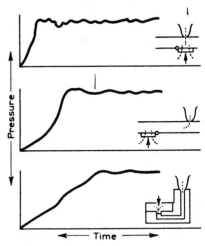

Fig 13   Influence of air valves on inflow of wind

the geometry of a pipe and valve assembly can affect the starting of the sound, and in Fig. 14 we can see what actually happens on admission of the wind to a pipe—that is, after it has been through the valve passage.

We have instanced this starting transient as a function of the flue organ pipe, but it exists in any system set into forced vibration and is noticeable in struck or plucked strings. It can be eliminated by electrical means.

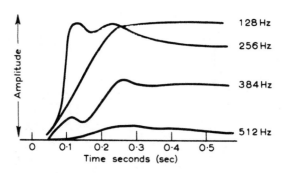

Fig 14   Relative rise time of harmonics in 128 Hz organ pipe

The pianoforte

Today we have a great number of electrical percussion circuits by means of which piano and similar effects can be synthesized, sometimes so well that they cannot be detected. Nevertheless, the total effect is not that of the piano, and perhaps we should see what makes the conventional piano sound as it does.

Generally, from tenor C upwards, there is little to distinguish one piano from another. It is in the bass that there is a great difference, and this is because of the size of the soundboard. Since we know that the strings themselves cannot radiate any energy, it is obvious that the larger the bass area of the soundboard, the better the effect on the ear. This explains the shape of the grand piano, and as we will see when we look at the sensitivity curves of the ear, much more energy is needed at the lower end of the compass to give equal loudness.

The frequencies of the partials of a struck string are not truly harmonics of the fundamental frequency, and such partials are progressively sharpened as their order increases. This "inharmonicity" is not the same for all strings, being least in the middle of the keyboard and increasing towards the bottom and the top. It is most pronounced at the upper end, and this is not

Fig 15   Mistuning between piano strings on striking a note C = 523 Hz

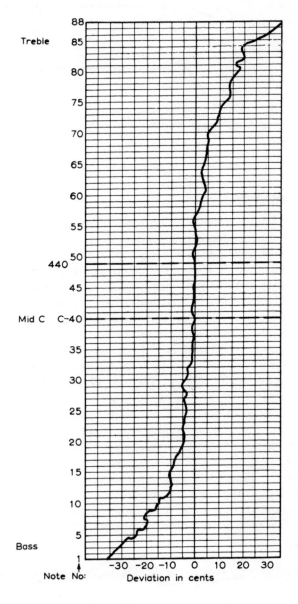

Fig 16   Piano tuning deviation

surprising since the top strings, being so short and stiff, are really more like bars than strings. Because of the differences in mass and tension, we find a mistuning effect as in Fig. 15 for an average grand piano, since tuners depend on the rate of beating of certain intervals for the accuracy of tempering the scale. This effect is very real as can be seen from Fig. 16 which shows the average of sixteen pianos examined. Note here that one cent is one hundredth of a semitone, so there are 1200 cents to an octave; one cent is equal to a frequency difference of 0·06%. For the reasons given, the effect of sustaining many consecutive chords in the extreme upper or lower registers would become displeasing in a very short time. With a long string, even when damped by the mechanism provided, the sound does not cease immediately, and when the dampers are removed by the sustaining pedal, the string may vibrate for a long time, as in Fig. 17. This is the Mid C string, but of course there are no

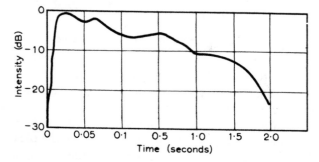

Fig 17   Decay curve for piano

single strings in the instrument, except in the bass, and the effect of the three strings settling down after striking is very complex, adding a further difficulty to any method of synthesis. Firstly they vibrate in phase, but soon they begin to vibrate in a random manner because the mass and tension cannot be exactly the same for every string. It is this kind of fractional deviation which gives the richness of tone to a good piano.

Now there is one very important characteristic of the piano, the percussive starting tone. Examination of a piano waveform always shows a very steep rise, of a transient nature, to the start of the wave. But the oscillations of the string do not contain any transients. The effect is due to a rotational movement of the bridge axis at the moment of striking the string, as a result of the sudden relief of strain in this member. That such a transient does exist is easily proved by electrical pickups. At no point on the string can this sharp impact sound be obtained, but if a pickup is placed on the bridge the sound becomes percussive, see Fig. 18.

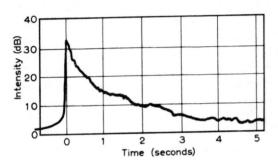

Fig 18   Percussive start of piano tone

"Electric" pianos have been made, in which the sound is removed from the strings by a series of pickups, but they do not sound very like pianos; it is necessary to have some sound-board to stop the strings from continuing to vibrate indefinitely, yet not enough to act as a loudspeaker to excite the pickups in a spurious manner. It is very difficult to play such a piano, examples of which were produced by Nernst, Bechstein, Vierling and Forster.

In considering the harp, the only real difference is the absence of a proper soundboard, requiring the strings to be stopped by hand. Otherwise the vibrations would persist for a long time, allowing notes to run into each other. The resultant tone quality depends very greatly on the point at which the string is plucked. If it were plucked in the centre, all even partials would be absent from the tone; if plucked at one seventh from the end, this and all other partials having a node at this point would be suppressed, and the tone would be smoother and more agree-able. Again, if the finger is used, the angle is less acute where the string is plucked than if a sharp point were used, therefore the latter would invoke a harder and more nasal tone.

The vibrations begin to die away as soon as the string is released, but the higher order ones decay much faster than the lower ones, so the sound appears more pleasant to the ear as it persists. Thus, the player has several ways of modifying the sound spectrum.

The glockenspiel

The glockenspiel, celesta and dulcitone represent types of percussion instrument using metal bars struck by hammers. Such bars must be thin compared with their vibrating length to ensure

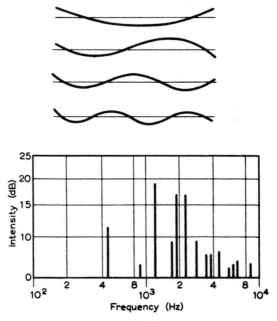

Fig 19   Spectrum of glockenspiel

they will only vibrate in one plane. Otherwise the tone quality is a very complex mixture of odd partials. Figure 19 shows a

free bar and the position of the first few overtones. The fundamental frequency of such a bar is

$$f_1 = \frac{1 \cdot 33}{l^2} \sqrt{\frac{QK^2}{p}}$$

where l is the length of bar in centimetres; p is the density,
grammes per cubic centimetre; Q is the Young's modulus,
dynes per **square** centimetre; and K is the radius of gyration.

For a rectangular cross-section,

$$K = \pm a/\sqrt{12}$$

where a is the thickness of the bar in centimetres.

The bar is of course supported at the two nodes nearest to the
free ends, usually on small pads of felt or by cords, and struck
at the centre. The fundamental is very weak when mounted
on a frame in free air, owing to the small size of the radiating
area compared with a wavelength. As the rate of exchange of
operating force is great, owing to the hard hammers, the sound
starts instantly and is very incisive. The bars being stiff, the
vibrations decay rapidly too.

Atonal instruments

These are used as rhythm markers and are not music makers but
noise generators. Their chief characteristic is an immediate and
percussive attack, with various forms of decay curve, but most
may be sustained by reiteration, that is, constantly hitting the
device to keep it vibrating.

The triangle is a steel bar of circular section bent into the
form of a triangle, but not completely closed. The cross-section may vary throughout the length of the bar. From its
construction, it is obvious that it can vibrate transversely,
longitudinally or torsionally, and all these vibrations may
super-impose themselves on one another. The net result is a
closely packed vibration pattern of high partials (there can be
no low ones on account of the short length of the bar), and
these are both harmonic and inharmonic. It is largely because
there are so many high inharmonic tones that the triangle can

be heard above a full orchestra, since there are gaps in the total sound spectrum into which these partials can obtrude. Somewhat similar sounds can be synthesized quite well; they are not the same but quite acceptable.

The cymbal is the other important rhythm marker, also a noise generator; but the partials are of a quite different kind. The circular brass plate is supported at the centre, which must then be a node for all vibrations. The diameter is considerable, producing a large sound output in the high frequency range; by far the largest amount of energy is radiated from 5000 Hz upwards, indeed, far above audibility. The vibrations of the plate are very complex and are always inharmonic; it would be possible to vibrate the plate in one of its major modes if it were perfectly balanced and of uniform stress distribution. There is no real steady state for the sound, even with reiteration, but it can be analysed and a part of its spectrum is shown in Fig. 20.

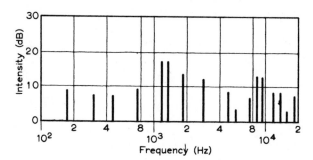

Fig 20   Spectrum of cymbal at frequency of 175 Hz

Synthesis yields a very tolerable imitation, but it is only acceptable in the absence of the original. The power output in the range shown is so great that a single cymbal will stand out loud and clear above the orchestra; but enclosure or shielding of the instrument will remove the upper overtones, as indeed is the case with most musical instruments.

It is of interest to note the peak power outputs of some of the more common orchestral instruments. This gives a clue as to possible electrical powers required for simulation; if one takes the efficiency of a really good loudspeaker properly mounted at 10%, then amplifiers having continuous power ratings of ten times the figures shown would be satisfactory. Usually additional power is in reserve in case of difficult acoustic conditions. See Table 1.

Table 1   Peak powers over the whole spectrum

Source	Power, watts
75 piece orchestra	75
15 in. cymbal	9·5
trombone	6·5
trumpet	0·6
violincello	0·16
flute	0·06
French horn	0·05
clarinet	0·05
triangle	0·05

2 Musical scales, temperament and tuning; concord and discord

Generally, sounds which are smooth, regular, pleasant and harmonious, and which either together or singly appeal to the ear may be classed as musical. But certain sounds of the same nature sounded together may give rise to an unpleasant sensation. We call the former concordant, the latter discordant. The octave is the basis for measurement and although only containing 12 notes, has been subdivided into 1200 parts called cents to attain some degree of accuracy. There are accordingly 100 cents to the semitone, which is the smallest interval of the musical scale for Western countries and the smallest which can conveniently be written on paper.

No conventional musical sound has any value unless it contains some harmonics as well as the fundamental or pitch note. These harmonics should arise naturally from the vibratile characteristics of the instrument, and the most accurate and pleasing ones derive from a stretched string. If this is bowed correctly, analysis shows that the tones engendered are in the ratios 1, 2, 3, 4, 5, 6 etc; this is called a harmonic series. If the bowing is continuous, at all other frequency intervals there are discordant sounds, which vanish at the exact points where the frequency ratios are found to be 5:4, 4:3, 3:2 and 2:1. It is a general law that two tones sound well together when the ratios of their frequencies can be expressed in small numbers. If we look at Table 2, we can see the increasing dissonance, so that the further we go from small numbers, the worse the discord.

Table 2 Frequency ratio versus dissonance

Note	Frequency ratio	ET interval error, cents	
C	1	0	0
D	9:8	200	4♭
E	5:4	400	14#
F	4:3	500	2#
G	3:2	700	2♭
A	5:3	900	16#
B	15:8	1100	12#
C	2:1	1200	0

The well-known dissonance curve of von Helmholtz shows this perhaps more clearly, Fig. 21, where one violin sounds c_1

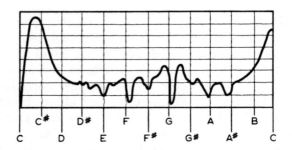

Fig 21   Helmholtz dissonance curve

continuously whilst the other one moves gradually from c_1 to c_2.

Evidently the only two tones which cannot introduce any possible disturbance are those of the octave, which is the ratio 2:1. The tones which are the next most agreeable have frequencies in the ratio 3:2, or, 1·5. Thus, sounding one pair of such notes would be agreeable, and so would one or two more pairs; but eventually, as we have 12 notes in the octave, if we increased each step (or note) by the factor 1·5, we would have a value of 129·5. This is not exactly the value of the note (c) constituting the octave, it should be 128. Now we are a quarter of a semitone too high, and if this were continued, we would find that still higher notes ran far away from true pitch and resulted in discord. So some other solution must be sought. Neglecting the various mean tone and other methods of scaling which were in use at one time, the solution was found to lie in equal temperament tuning (which was proposed as long ago as 1482). Now, to obtain a frequency ratio of 128:1, each step must represent one twelfth of that, $\sqrt[12]{128}$ or 1·4983. All semitones are now equal, and each represents exactly the same frequency ratio. Within an octave this is the twelfth root of two, or 1·05945.

Now clearly some intervals must still sound better than others, and in certain keys there may be a loss of purity as compared with the mean tone or just scale; that this is a very real effect is shown by the scaling adopted by violinists and many vocalists; continuous monitoring of the spectrum shows these performers to depart from the equal scale to a considerable extent to secure purity of tone. Of course, in tuning certain instruments having keyboards, e.g., the piano and the organ, there may well be further stretching of the intervals to modify the effect of dissonant harmonics in the instrument.

We have devoted some space to these matters because it must be clear that to synthesize musical sound by the addition of sine waves tuned to the intervals of the equally tempered scale would lead to very dubious results after the 6th harmonic. A third for example is a ratio of 1·2599, but a true third is 1·250; the tempered fifth is 1·4983, and is low in the ratio 1·4983:1·5 or approximately 881:882. Naturally, the sound from any instrument rich in harmonics would greatly complicate the above, which are related to pure waves only. It is clearly possible by electronic means to provide tone sources where the intervals could be flattened or sharpened at will, indeed it is only where conventional keyboards, wind valves or holes etc., are concerned, that the equal temperament scale need apply. When one looks at this convention, it is apparent that the real reason for the intervals as we know them is to allow a human being to span the controlling apparatus comfortably. Twelve keys to the octave are satisfactory; 25 keys would not be possible. But there is no limit to the gradations of the scale where electronic music is concerned. Any possible limitation is only because of the difficulty of committing the music to paper. As we shall see later, this is by no means necessary in all cases.

It has, in fact, been proposed to have a 53 note scale, which would give true fifths as well as all the other intervals, including the all-important third. But even this is slightly imperfect and this is only the more reason why electronic frequencies should be generated as continuous gliding tones, to be dissected and combined as required. There are ways of annotating this kind of spectrum, although perhaps not immediately intelligible; but then, is conventional music intelligible to anyone not trained to interpret it?

The various ways of notationally conveying the composers' intentions to the performer as employed in conventional music scores may prove to be totally inadequate where electronic music is concerned. This is because, for the first time, the limits imposed by the construction and use of physical instruments have been removed. At the same time, there may be complications attached to any new form of notation because it will be in the form of "machine language," i.e., instructions relating to one particular device or system and therefore not common to all methods. Just as an elementary illustration, the information for computer produced music will be totally different from that for a manual system.

Any programming information, to be complete, must include the basic parameters of any musical sound, because unlike conventional instruments a programme does not start with a complete tone colour but with the separate ingredients. Therefore, any notation of real merit must include means for indicating frequency, intensity, duration, envelope, harmonics, possible noise, and mode of attack and decay (which might be contained in the envelope control). All of these could have infinite gradations, so clearly a notation must be worked out for the complexity of the system. So, for the time being at least, we can regard any written notation system as temporary and probably unsuitable for many synthesis machines.

All the foregoing values can be represented digitally, but we are faced with a difficulty in regard to time intervals, which must be shown in analogue. Nevertheless, the time factor is one of the most important and is related to the envelope and duration factors. One simple way of conveying some of the information in a continuous way is that of the Cologne school of electronic music. This applies to manually operated apparatus, therefore the information (in this example) is limited to the capability of two hands, the intensity being controlled by the foot. Only the frequency, duration and intensity are shown in Fig. 22, the reason being that this is the information for one

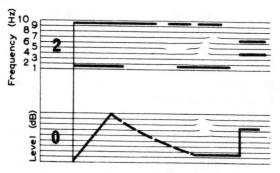

Fig 22   Proposed notation system

operator, the balance of the parameters either being provided by other operators at the same time, or introduced by re-recording afterwards. All the same, a composer could at least deduce the melodic content from the example, sufficiently extended in time.

It will be evident later that each system must have its own method of programming, if only for the simple reason that each system is different mechanically and electrically. Whilst, therefore, we have devoted space to the definition of matters like frequency, scaling and tuning, this is merely to provide reference points to which a return can be made as a check. Although if one of the purposes envisaged by the reader is investigation into the properties of conventional musical instruments, then this information will be required.

Before passing to tuning, it might be as well to look at some other parameters of musical sounds. Firstly, *pitch*.

Pitch is related to the frequency of a fundamental tone. It is subjective in character; in other words, the assessment of an exact pitch depends on the judgement or acuity of perception of individual persons. The relation to frequency is not a linear function, a pitch interval being representative not of a specific difference, but of a specific ratio of frequencies. The logarithm of the frequency shares with the pitch the property that, on an alteration of the sound by the same pitch interval, it always increases by the same amount, irrespective of the absolute frequency values:

$$\log (f_1/f_2) = \log f_1 - \log f_2$$

A reasonably acute ear can distinguish about one thousand four hundred distinct pitch intervals in fact. Since there are only a hundred and twenty discrete tones in the ET scale, the perception of the ear is much in excess of ordinary musical requirements. Accurate pitch judgement depends very much on the loudness and harmonic texture of the sound. This brings us to the very important question of loudness, which again is a physical interpretation of a particular kind and amount of sound intensity. But this time it is harder to find a basis for accurate comparison within the structure of the tone itself. Observations carried out on many listeners show that the ratio I_2/I_1 of the sound intensities between which the ear can just differentiate is constant over a wide range and is approximately 1·2.

To be able to give a numerical value to the differences in intensity we adopt the decibel (db). The difference in level between two powers or intensities is n decibels where

$$n = 10 \log (W_2/10W_1) \qquad \text{or} \qquad W_2/W_1 = 10^{10/n}$$

If it is remembered that $\log 2 = 0·030$ and that 1 db corresponds to an energy increase of approximately 25%, the intensity ratio corresponding to a specific number of db can then be found. Of course, a reference power level must be taken for W_1 above, and this is usually 0 db $= 10^{-16}$ watts per square centimetre, or 0·0002 dynes per square cm. We therefore show the Fletcher-Munson hearing curves in Fig. 23, with the area usefully occupied by music within the range of loudness which the ear can accept. It has already been pointed out that the apparent loudness depends greatly on the complexity or otherwise of the sound; it should be noted that this figure relates to pure or single tones only. If the tones in the region 2000–4000 Hz were complex, they would sound much louder than shown.

A sound cannot be instantly identified; many investigators have examined the time necessary to definitely establish a sense of pitch. There is good agreement regardless of the kind of sound, and it is found that 12 to 14 milliseconds is necessary. A shorter period of time induces a sense of irritation, since the ear has a longer resolving time. Figure 24 shows the required time against frequency.

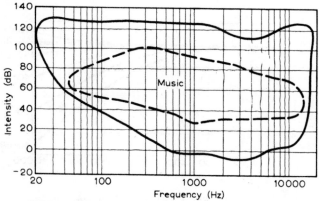

Fig 23   Limits of audibility with music area in centre

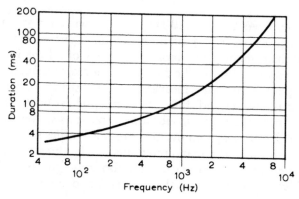

Fig 24   Pitch identification graph

It is as well to remember that as we get older, we begin to lose response to the higher frequencies. This is quite marked after some 45 years of age, the effect as measured on a large number of groups of men and women being shown in Fig. 25.

It is clear that the usual concept of tuning, as applied to a piano, may well not apply at all to electronic tone producers. Nevertheless, they must all have a reference or primary pitch tone, since otherwise it would not be possible to re-record with other instruments or synthesizers—and little is possible in this art without re-recording. For many years the standard pitch

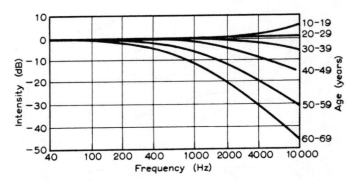

Fig 25   Hearing loss with age

has been fixed at A = 440 Hz, and this will soon spread to all countries. However, to maintain the tonal virtues of some keyboard instruments, the absolute accuracy of all the intervals is not the same. This may be due to various reasons, but in the case of the piano (where it is most obvious), the strings really become bars at the upper end, they are so stiff; whilst at the bass end, the wrapping alters their vibrating properties so that there is a kind of 3 tuning system overall. From a synthesis aspect, there is no such thing as a piano pitch merely changing progressively over the compass; the harmonics also undergo great changes, being very prominent at the bass end and nonexistent at the treble end.

To conclude this chapter, we give as Table 3 a frequency table covering the majority of discrete pitches required for tonal synthesis. This is of course based on the equally tempered scale and does not provide for any stretching or other adjustment of the intervals.

Table 3 Frequency table,* Hz

C	C#	D	D#
16·351	17·323	18·354	19·445
32·703	34·647	36·708	38·890
65·406	69·295	73·416	77·781
130·812	138·591	146·832	155·563
261·625	277·182	293·664	311·126
523·251	554·365	587·329	622·253
1046·502	1108·730	1174·059	1244·507
2093·004	2217.460	2344·318	2489·014
4186·008	4434·920	4698·636	4978·028
8372·016	8869·840	9397·272	9956·056
16744·032			

E	F	F#	G
20·601	21·826	23·124	24·499
41·203	43·653	46·249	48·999
82·406	87·307	92·498	97·998
164·813	174·614	184·997	195·997
329·627	349·228	369·994	391·995
659·255	698·456	739·988	783·991
1318·510	1396·912	1479·976	1567·982
2637·020	2793·824	2959·952	3135·964
5274·040	5587·648	5919·904	6270·928
10548·080	11175·296	11839·808	12541·856

G#	A	A#	B
25·956	27·500	29·135	30·867
51·913	55·000	58·270	61·735
103·826	110·000	116·540	123·470
207·652	220·000	233·081	246·941
415·304	440·000	466·163	493·883
830·609	880·000	932·327	987·766
1661·218	1760·000	1864·654	1975·532
3322·436	3520·000	3729·308	3951·064
6644·872	7040·000	7458·616	7902·128
13289·744	14080·000	14917·232	15804·256

CCCC 16·351 Hz is the lowest note of 32 ft pitch.
CCC   32·703 Hz is the lowest note of 16 ft pitch.
CC   65·406 Hz is the lowest note of 8 ft pitch.
C   261·625 Hz is the so-called middle C of the keyboard.

* Reproduced from *Electronic Music Instrument Manual*, Sir Isaac Pitman & Sons Ltd, London, 1969.

3 Electronic music generators

Since there is an infinite variety of musical forms, ranging from the simple melodic line to the most complex orchestration, there must correspondingly be an infinite number of ways or devices for generating the required sound spectrum. Accordingly, we will look first at simple machines, because even with the most elementary apparatus it is possible to re-record again and again and thus build up a complex spectrum. It is largely a matter of purpose, convenience, skill and cost. The private investigator of limited means need not be at a disadvantage with the university or commercial recording company in this matter. But where the individual may score is in having the facility to imitate any sound regardless of his ability or otherwise to play an instrument, and to be able to set up any combination of sounds at the cost of a few reels of tape. A composer can have copies made for transmission to interested parties, who can then play these back anywhere in the world. How else could this be done except through the medium of electronics?

We know the basic parameters for forming a musical sound; we also know that noise can be a useful adjunct if properly controlled. So let us look at apparatus capable of being constructed at low cost and operated by one person. Now it has been stated that all the parameters to compound a sound should be produced independently, then processed as may be required. But obviously this is a method demanding fairly complex equipment. It is going to be difficult not to introduce aspects of composition or musical form in this kind of discussion, but for the moment we must leave this aspect.

In the average electronic organ, waveforms having known characteristics are generated and processed to give sustained or perhaps percussive sounds. The only difference in this case being that there are fixed tonal intervals because of the use of a keyboard, whereas we want a continuous frequency range. So, if we are prepared to accept fixed kinds of tone colour, we can use a multivibrator as in Fig. 26. Here we can see that instead

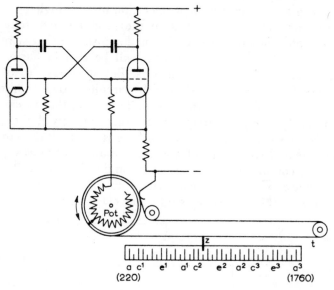

Fig 26   Stepless waveform generator

of key or switches, there is a cord which can be pulled by a ring along a calibrated scale, on which any instructions as to pitch may be written. If the variable element in the multivibrator is logarithmic, then the scale may be linear, which prevents crowding at one end.

The pulley is returned by a spring, so that the operator must always have tension on the ring. Naturally, the frequency spectrum produced is continuous, even if arrested at any position of the scale, therefore a means to stop the signal until required is necessary. This can be a foot switch, a variable resistance strip beneath the scale, or a photoelectric device actuated by displacing the cord front to rear. There are many other methods which could be employed. The waveform obtained without treatment would be square, that is, containing a wide range of odd harmonics only. It could be modified in re-recording and at the same time, the shape of the onset and cessation of the sound could be changed. But, gliding tones can be produced by this simple machine, not possible with any keyboard instrument.

It will be appreciated that operation of any single oscillator system or circuit must result in the production of only one pitch note, though if the device is; for instance, like a multi-vibrator, the resultant waveforms will be rich in harmonics, which introduce other frequencies. But it is easy to obtain octaves of the fundamental pitch by circuits known as bistable frequency dividers, and these being aperiodic, that is, capable of dividing almost any frequency fed in, can follow gliding tones etc. Moreover, the waveform resulting is virtually the same as from the multivibrator and is a substantially square wave, Fig. 27. This contains no even harmonics, and if these are called for, the square wave can be converted into an almost linear saw-tooth wave, which contains odd and even harmonics in their

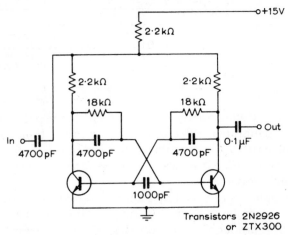

Fig 27   Bistable frequency divider

correct order and amplitude, by means of the circuit shown in Fig. 28. Of course, if only fixed frequency intervals are desired, the bistable circuits could be arranged to divide by some other integer than 2. The use of this kind of circuit means that only one controlling device may be required, since if bistables are

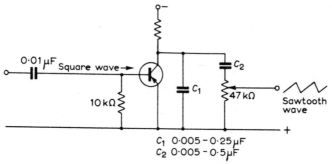

Fig 28   Sawtooth converter

connected in cascade, they will automatically turn on and off when the actual oscillators are energized or cut off. Detailed constructional information on this kind of circuit is to be found in most books dealing with electronic organs. Many present day integrated circuits are also available for this purpose.

An alternative is to use a beat frequency oscillator, one of the oscillators having a logarithmically shaped capacitor also operated by a cord. One of the parameters which is not basic but often desirable, namely vibrato, can be inserted during these operations. It could be continuous and of uniform intensity, as in an electronic organ, or it might be made variable; for instance, the plate on which the scale for playing is laid out can be on rollers, so that a slight to and fro movement is possible. The action can be used to control some means of changing the basic frequency. A spring must always return the roller to a known position. By careful finger action, a vibrato similar to that of a 'cello player can be obtained, an artistic effect if properly used. The more change of basic pitch which can be introduced at any one time, the less need for re-recording. With the simple device outlined above, one can then obtain a complex wave of any pitch, a variation in volume or loudness, and a vibrato of possibly a variable nature all at the one time, leaving only the shaping of the front and rear of the signal to be performed afterwards. It may appear a great limitation to be able to produce only one line of music at a time, but even with the most complex manually operated gear, it is rarely possible to produce more than two parts at any one time.

It will be evident that the operation of a multivibrator like this only requires one hand, so that shaping circuits could perhaps be controlled by the other; this is a matter of acquired skill and not a technical limitation. A method which has been used, for instance, is shown in Fig. 29. Here we assume that the generator is able to supply more than one waveform for any note

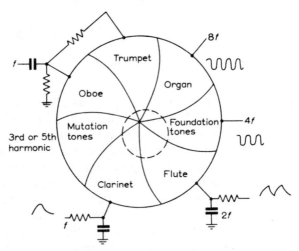

Fig 29   Waveform controller

simultaneously. This is quite easy if conventional tone filter circuits are applied to the source, that is, the square wave. The signals so derived could be square, sine and sawtooth, and these are taken to the mixer element shown in the figure. This simple but ingenious device consists of a series of metal segments, all insulated from each other but mounted on a common bakelite plate, one waveform being connected to each segment. If now a metal disc about the proportions shown is covered with a thin layer of plastic on one side, so that there is no metallic contact with the segmented disc, then if the circular plate is laid on, say, the sine segment, a wave of that shape will be transmitted through capacitive coupling to a subsequent amplifier. If the disc is moved to another segment, that particular wave will be transmitted; if it overlaps two segments, a composite wave is available; if the disc is moved away from the segments, the volume will alter in a square law fashion. So, by careful manipulation of the circular disc, a great many effects are possible. This could be (and has been) operated by the left hand. Thus, in the foregoing inexpensive device, are the elements of a music synthesizer of quite a potent nature.

But there are times when it is required to produce a sine wave, either for use as generated or for forming other sounds by addition of similar waves. It must by this time be understood that additive synthesis can only be carried out with pure sinusoids, although this does not prevent the addition of harmonically rich waveforms for special or grotesque effects. One may ask why there is this kind of difficulty, and the answer is that sum and difference tones are produced by the interaction of harmonics or partials in the complex wave, and these further intermodulate with what we have to produce—unacceptable effects in the main. It is not very easy to cover a wide range of notes in a gliding manner with one stepless control if sine waves only are required and filtering must be applied to a square wave every two or three notes if this is the source for the sine wave. Phase shift oscillators are very suitable for sine wave generation, one variable circuit being shown in Fig. 30. The waveform improves as one approaches the threshold condition, that is, when the circuit will only just oscillate.

Long-term stability of either frequency or amplitude is not always required from circuits which are only in use for a matter of minutes at a time. Nevertheless, such attributes are desirable and although usually attainable only at some expense or complication, can be combined in a simple oscillator using a BIFET amplifier with an inductance; this latter confers stability and the former ensures reliable performance over a wide range of voltage and temperature changes. If we look at Fig. 31, the Philips type TAA 320 device provides a field-effect transistor and a high-gain bipolar transistor all in the one TO-18 case.

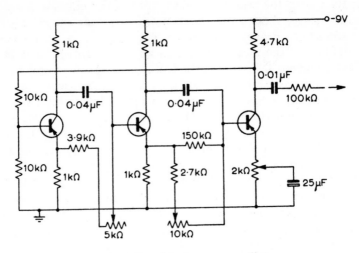

Fig 30   Adjustable sine wave oscillator

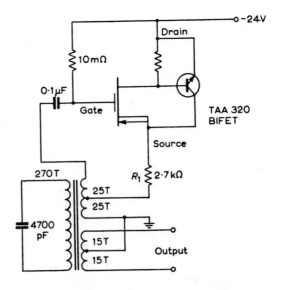

Fig 31   High stability sine wave oscillator

The high gate impedance allows the use of a high Q tank circuit, thus almost eliminating output distortion. The waveform is sinusoidal and the harmonic distortion is less than 0·1 %. With a 24 volt supply rail, the oscillator output is 1·5 volts RMS into a 3000 ohm load, and since the Vinkor shown can provide a Q approaching 400, it is easy to attain the 10 (minimum) called for. R_1 limits the current and could be adjusted. As shown, the frequency is 10 KHz and changes in supply of up to 25 % cause no measurable output changes. Of course, this design is intended for fixed frequency operation but can be made extremely compact and is recommended for very high stability over a long period.

Reverting for a moment to the case of sum and difference frequencies, if for example two musical instruments of widely differing harmonic content or waveform play two contrasting chords simultaneously, then according to the relative position of the pitch notes, the harmonics would beat in quite different ways. Note how this is determined by the harmonic ratios of the pitch note, expressed as intervals. Thus, unusual results from the synthesis of complex waveforms may be very misleading, and this is one reason why sine waves are to be preferred, at least for a start. See Fig. 32.

In fact, the only feature of a sound which cannot be simulated, apart from the admixture of noise, is a percussive attack

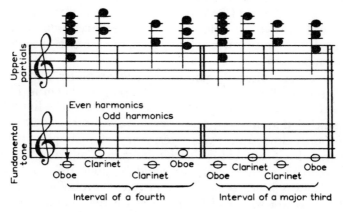

Fig 32   Beats due to unequal harmonic texture

or decay. One can obtain an abrupt start or stop by means of a switch but this is not the same. Apart from its invariable nature, it must introduce a click—one cannot cut into a sustained frequency without transients being formed. Therefore shaping must be resorted to, unless a satisfactory technique of manipulation for the cord is developed. The shaping does not substantially alter the waveshape in the sense that it does not remove or add harmonics; but it will alter their relative intensity and for this reason it may be best to treat a sine wave only in any shaping circuits—certainly to begin with. Also, this enables one to observe the shaping effect much more accurately, since it is a pure tone and there are no harmonics to confuse the effect.

The number of shaping circuits, or envelope control devices, is legion; but this is due mostly to commercial considerations, sometimes involving patents. The experimenter can choose between those shown later in Figs. 39–52, which are adequate for most effects.

In the foregoing apparatus we have assumed simplicity and small bulk. This may result in certain disadvantages. For instance, it is well known that extending controls which carry signals can lead to hum pickup, attenuation or distortion of the frequency band. It may well be necessary to control the gain of amplifiers or the frequency of oscillators from a distance or by a method which follows some law, e.g., linear or logarithmic. Moreover, it would be extremely convenient if the devices for control were very simple and could be divorced from the actual signal equipment which they control. This is possible by voltage control.

One could alter the gain of an audio amplifier, for example, with a metal oxide field effect transistor as shown in Fig. 33. This is a simple example with a simple example's limitations, namely, that at very large levels there is considerable distortion. Below 50 millivolts it works very well, a simple potentiometer with a 3 volt battery varies the gain of any amplifier from zero to maximum, and this could be done from a hundred yards away if necessary. However, the control of gain is linear, which is not so useful for music since the loudness increases logarithmically, or very nearly so. Therefore it would be

desirable to convert the linear change in voltage into a logarithmic change in voltage, and this can be done by circuits taking
advantage of the exponential volt-ampere characteristics of
some diodes which have this feature; the 4JA10A is one such.
At the same time, and since this form of control can be applied
to other music devices, like oscillators, filters etc., it is clear that
some of these could be controlled by signals from more than

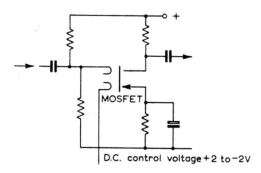

Fig 33   Simple voltage control

one source, so a linear adding circuit can be designed to produce a voltage which is proportional to the sum of all the input
voltages, and which can then be attached to an exponential
converter which produces a current proportional to the ex-
ponent of the sum of the input voltages—such voltages coming
from different control devices. For instance, one of the voltage
inputs might be a series of tappings on a linear voltage divider,
which would produce the intervals of the equally tempered
scale if the driven device was an oscillator. Vibrato could be
applied to another input, whilst the third could be used for
special effects; for example, transient frequency changes.

A simple example of voltage control is of course the vibrato
circuit of an electronic organ, where the voltage change across
a resistor is applied to the base of oscillators; as this swings
about, so does the frequency of these oscillators. The method is
also used to effect permanent changes in frequency, for example
in some Conn organs, the base bias voltage on alternate
oscillators is altered by means of a switch and different values of

resistor, in order to slightly detune these oscillators and so give a chorus effect when many are combined.

The effect of simple voltage control can be enhanced if the swing so engendered is amplified before being used. An example of this can be seen in Fig. 34. This is a multivibrator in which

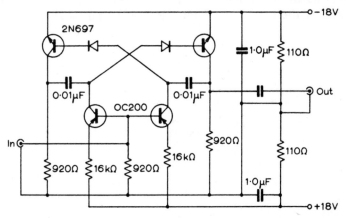

Fig 34   Simple voltage control multivibrator

two transistors replace the customary base to 0 volt resistors. The current flowing through these is controlled by the input voltage applied where shown. Silicon transistors are desirable from a stability aspect, and the required + and − voltages are probably best derived from a single 18 volt supply as indicated. The maximum control voltage will be about half the line voltage, and this can be applied through a wire-wound potentio-meter. But of course, AC signal voltages from audio sources can be applied in the form of a voltage swing as well, modulating the existing frequency of the multivibrator and leading to many remarkable effects since one frequency will be superimposed on the other and as the voltage is altered, a chord is formed which can be made to rise and fall over a wide range. In Fig. 35 we show one circuit which can be used for adding and feeding the diode groups which are required for the exponential function. The ratio R_2/R_1 determines the proportionality relating the output voltage to the sum of the input voltages. This output is in series with the first group of series diodes, whilst a fixed

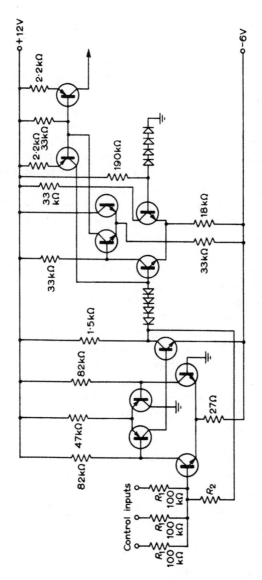

Fig 35   Adder and exponential generator

current is passed through the second group. Since the amplifier is differential, an appropriate current must be applied to the first series of diodes to minimize the voltage difference between the positive ends of the two sets of diodes. This value can be found mathematically.

The purpose of this unit is to feed an oscillator in which a unijunction transistor acts as a sawtooth generator. One such circuit is given in Fig. 36, attributed to R. A. Moog. Such relaxation oscillators are quite common, but this one has some interesting features. The current mentioned above for the diodes is supplied by one of a matched pair of transistors; the other supplies the same amount of current to the control terminal of the oscillator. Since this oscillator depends on the charging time of a capacitor for its frequency accuracy, if the supply voltage is regulated, the frequency of oscillation will be proportional to the control current and inversely proportional to the size of the charging capacitor. The control current must not be so large as to cause the unijunction to fire continuously. The total range of the circuit can be extended by switching in extra capacitors as shown. With 0·015 mfd in circuit, the circuit as shown will reach 8 kHz, and with the 2·4 mfd capacitor, the frequency range is from 0·2 to 50 Hz.

However, other operations are carried out in this circuit. After the unijunction buffer stage there is a wave shaper. This transistor has large resistors in both the emitter and collector circuits. The bias states are so arranged that the transistor saturates at the mid point of the applied sawtooth. This ensures that before saturation, the collector voltage falls as the emitter voltage rises. After saturation, both these voltages rise together. Thus, the emitter waveform is still a sawtooth, but the collector waveform is triangular as in Fig. 37. After suitable filtering, the waveform is as shown at the bottom of the figure—very suitable for use as a basic music waveform, having a flute-like sound.

Both the sawtooth wave and the triangular one are isolated by emitter followers. The sawtooth is also applied to a clipper, which switches rapidly from non-conducting to a fully saturated state. The resulting pulse is controlled in width by the 5 k pot from 5 % to 50 % of the period.

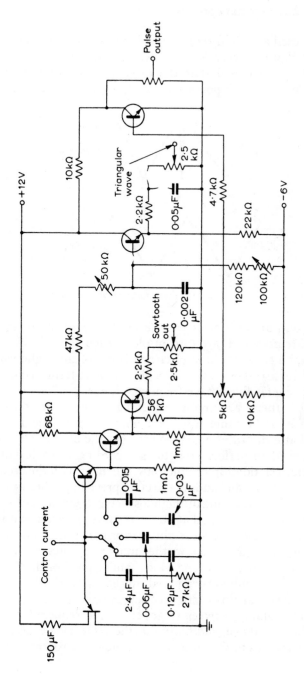

Fig 36 Voltage controlled oscillator

This oscillator is direct coupled, which means that it can operate down to very low frequencies indeed. Moreover, the outputs are so biased that the extreme negative part of the waveform is at earth potential, which of course means that any

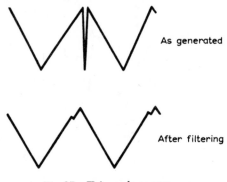

As generated

After filtering

Fig 37   Triangular wave

of the output waveforms can be used as control voltages for other circuits which are susceptible to such control. The long-term stability of this kind of circuit is not of the highest order, but with care it is possible to obtain short-term accuracy of $\pm 0 \cdot 1\%$ over a five octave frequency range.

Again, there are many advantages from controlling an amplifier in the same way. Not only is the problem of gain control at a distance readily solved, but the control circuit can be designed to perform functions according to some voltage/ frequency relationship or other law. Then, as with the oscillator just described, an adding circuit preceding the amplifier permits of several control methods being applied at the same time. It is in this way that the versatility of electronic music systems so greatly exceeds the performance of conventional instruments. Figure 38 shows the circuit of a voltage-controlled amplifier, again after R. A. Moog, and typical of the facilities required in a fully-coordinated music system. Many other designs exist, but this is not a constructional book.

Direct coupling between stages ensures a frequency response from d.c. to above audibility; further, the range of control voltages extends to the same degree. These control relationships

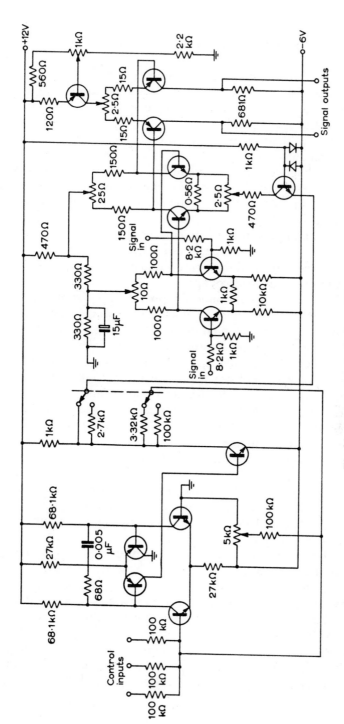

Fig 38 Voltage controlled amplifier

are of two kinds, linear and exponential. It has already been explained that the apparent or subjective sensation of loudness of an audible signal is approximately proportional to the exponential of the amplitude, so that a given change in control voltage would seem to change the loudness of the signal the same amount over a wide range of average loudness. Thus a linear voltage change as might be obtained from a simple potentiometer can be used to produce equal increments of loudness, as follows. When the mode switch of the adder circuit in Fig. 25g is in the exponential position, the output of the adder is applied to the base-emitter diode of a current supply transistor. Because of the characteristic of this diode, the collector current is almost proportional to the exponential of the sum of the control voltages.

A linear control position is also provided, this routes the output of the adder through a high value resistor, giving a collector current nearly proportional to the adder output voltage.

The amplifier proper consists of matched pairs of transistors, as it is completely balanced. This ensures that the average standing current will not appear in the output, but only the output current difference. An output impedance of about 600 ohms matches standard line transformers and is useful for many other purposes. If the circuit is carefully set up and there is good transistor matching, the balancing will be almost perfect. The voltage control method could be applied to other types of amplifier quite well, especially those circuits where the input or output impedances could vary with the gain or power; for with voltage control, this does not occur. Further, the control voltages do not themselves produce any signal at either the input or the output.

In the foregoing, no mention has been made of means to adjust the control voltages, beyond a tapped potentiometer. One could use anything suitable, for example a keyboard for many discrete intervals; or for gliding tones or infinite gain control a sliding resistor of the type invented by F. Trautwein in 1928 and used on the Trautonium (British Patents 380470 and 403365). In passing, the Trautonium was a voltage-controlled sawtooth oscillator system having facilities for gliding tones, on which a great deal of research into electronic music was carried out in Germany at Cologne. It is still used for recitals with or without an orchestra. Modern production techniques have evolved resistance materials with improved signal to noise characteristics and smaller bulk. Photocells can be used as a voltage control source, receiving information from a moving masking system. This can be seen in the Oramic sound synthesizer, later. These methods appear alarming to a musician, largely because there are no visible keys, switches or other well-understood means of operation. But anyone undertaking electronic music research must learn to understand the control functions and their realization; this is one of the penalties to pay for introducing a new art form. Fortunately, the effect of manipulating any of the controls is immediately audible, and in this way the musician will very soon find his way about. Just as a pianist must practice to attain proficiency, so an operator of electronic equipment must practice this kind of skill. But the effort is all mental, not physical.

Let us revert now to the shaping circuits mentioned as being in Figs. 39–52.

The comparatively simple circuit shown in Fig. 39 slows down the rate at which the sound starts, and at the same time,

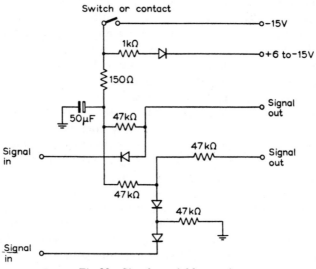

Fig 39   Simple variable sustain

introduces some delay in the cessation. Note that the signal source may run all the time, it is only when the switch is operated that a signal can pass out, because this applies +15 volts to the diode so forward biasing it to become conductive. At the same time, the 50 mfd capacitor is charged, even if the switch is touched momentarily, so the sound will decay slowly. This can be regulated by the 1 k resistor. Various times are possible by alteration of the bias between −15 and +6 volts. The second diode isolates one circuit from the other, so that more than one input signal could be treated at the same time. Quite long decays, up to 3 seconds, are obtainable from this very simple circuit. The overall time constant is a function of the product of R and C.

Percussive effects are of great value in music. When one considers the paucity of conventional instruments for this purpose, one can see a great many gaps into which all kinds of percussive sounds, both musical and atonal, could fit. Because of the comparatively long resolving time of the ear, there is a limit to the shortness of a percussive signal. It is well known for example that the ear only hears part of the sound of firing a pistol; but for music, times associated with the celeste or glockenspiel are very acceptable. The absolute value of these times are not at all important unless the score calls for this. So one of the most useful percussion circuits is given in Fig. 40 in the figure.

The principle of operation is as follows. The signal to be processed is fed into the two-stage amplifier 602, 603. The amplified signal then passes via the light dependent resistor 412 to the output. 412 is supplied with pulses by the lamp LA1 which is driven by the monostable circuit 405, 406. Negative going pulses are supplied from a manually operated contact driving 403. This circuit normally provides two rates of attack shape, but can be made to run freely at speeds determined by R 574. This produces reiteration, on a sine wave the effect is that of a banjo or mandoline. The performance of the circuit is dependent on the characteristics of the lamp and light dependent resistor, and some experiment may be necessary. Generally a 6 volt 0·04 amp lamp will be suitable. No special kind of contact is required to start this circuit, any kind will do.

Another way to control the waveform envelope is to use a

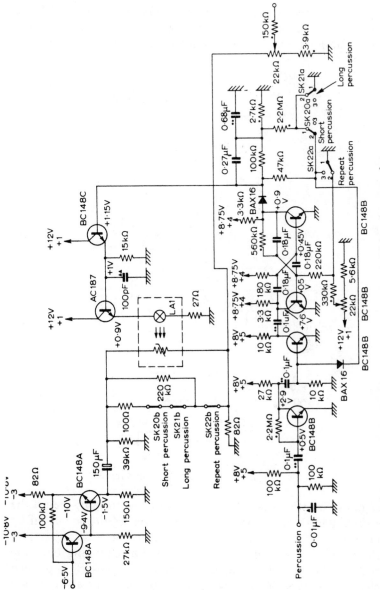

Fig 40 Complete percussion circuit. Symbol ▲ in Figure denotes tolerance:
▲ = 5% ▲▲ = 10%, etc.

tone gate of the kind shown in Fig. 41. Here a push–pull circuit is used, otherwise there would be a thump when the switch was operated. It could of course be transistorized if required. The explanation is easier if we consider valves. Assume the input

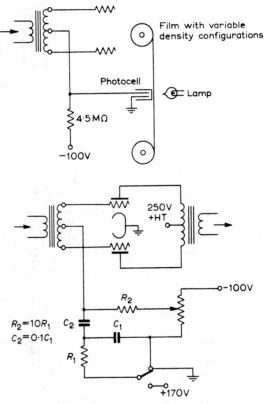

Fig 41   Envelope shaping circuits

signal to be of constant intensity at any one instant, then if the switch is in the position shown, the valves would be cut off by an excessive bias of about −90 volts on the grids; therefore there can be no signal at the output. On changing over the switch, the grid bias rapidly rises above cut-off and then charges the capacitors; it will return to −90 volts at some rate depending on the *RC* time constants.

During this time, the amplifier gain rises from zero to some value from which it then returns to zero, so that the input signal arrives at the output with its amplitude modulated in the shape of a bell. The width of the pulse can be adjusted by switching different values of C_1 and C_2. If the capacitors are shunted by suitably poled diodes they can discharge very quickly, then the circuit will be ready for use again on re-setting the switch. Naturally the maximum effect is produced on a sine wave.

The upper part of the figure shows a circuit for manual control, but it is possible to control the gate automatically by means of a photocell with suitable information applied in the form of opaque markings on a transparent moving film. Clearly this suggestion could operate manually or by any other means. For instance, a ratchet could advance the film as directed by a signal from some other part of the equipment or it could run continuously. Alternatively, it could merely have a number of preset masks. One can see that the optical method is capable of superimposing a pattern of control on any signal passing through the push–pull amplifier.

Discussion of percussion devices suggests rhythm and its processing for electronic music. Of course, since this is a non-musical marking system of sounds, there could be an infinite number of ways to produce it. However, we are not so much interested in the method for making rhythmic sounds as their introduction into other sound arrays or compositions. If the tempi employed are at all normal, then the noises used may be of conventional notation. But it is possible to automatically introduce noise and to do this at a rate far outside that at which a human being could operate any controls. By the use of a ring modulator controlled from a tape with suitable pulses thereon, one can introduce any kind of rhythmic pattern as follows.

A ring modulator is connected with a signal source, a suitable carrier frequency (above audibility) and tape player carrying pulses as required to form the rhythm. This tape is connected to the input terminals of the ring modulator, which will only pass the sound when carrier and signal frequency are applied simultaneously; the modulator has considerable stop-band attenuation against individually occurring frequencies. Now, if a series of pulses is applied to the tape loop in accordance with the desired rhythmic structure, the modulator will be blocked against the musical sound wherever the tape is free of impulses. In this way, any desired rhythmic pattern can be imposed on the sound. It is only necessary to ensure that the resulting products of modulation lie above the range of hearing (30 kHz has been used satisfactorily). See Fig. 42.

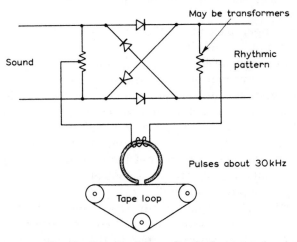

Fig 42   Ring modulator for rhythm control

All complex waveforms require to be modified since they either contain all the odd harmonics of the fundamental, or all the even harmonics; and there is no agreeable sound of this nature. Where sine waves are produced, other sine waves of the required intensity and frequency are added together to synthesize a tonecolour. But with complex waves, harmonics must be removed to form the desired spectrum. Filters are used for this purpose. As normally found on electronic organs, etc, each network represents a fixed tone quality and is not adjustable. But for electronic music synthesis or composition, one must have complete control over the filter action.

For the experimenter, quite simple circuits may suffice. In Fig. 43 we see a low pass filter, that is, the higher frequencies find it easy to escape to earth through the large capacitors, whilst the lower frequencies prefer to go through the circuits following. The degree of "smoothing" depends on the ratio of the time constant of the section to the input pulse length. Sections can be cascaded, that is, joined in series, with a progressive improvement in filtering, but with an increase in signal attenuation, as more series resistors are used. This loss can be greatly reduced by replacing the resistors by inductors, as shown in Fig. 44. If the resistive loss in the inductors is small,

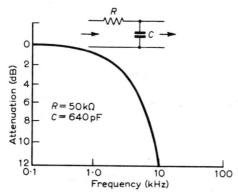

Fig 43   Low pass *RC* filter; theoretical cut-off $f = 1/(\omega RC)$

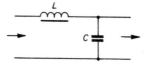

Fig 44   Low pass inductive filter

the resonance curve may be steep, in which case the filter will become very frequency selective and many sections of differing values will be required to cover a wide frequency range. It is generally better to arrange such an inductive filter in shunt, as in Fig. 45. Naturally, such a circuit is useful for making selected

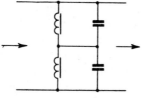

Fig 45   Band pass filter

frequencies prominent, for if the efficiency is high enough, the resonant frequency voltage can reach 30 or 40 times the applied voltage.

The circuit which performs the reverse function to Fig. 43 is shown at Fig. 46. This now prevents low frequencies from passing because the reactance of the very small capacitors is high.

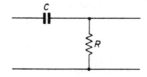

Fig 46   High pass filter

Again, for good smoothing there must be more than one section with corresponding losses as shown in Fig. 47. Adjustment of all these circuits is by altering one or more of the elements, all of

Fig 47   Increase of filtering and attenuation by increasing *C* of low pass filter

which carry some part of the a.c. signal. It would be much more convenient if the characteristics could be controlled progressively and over a wider range. Continuously adjustable filters have been developed many years ago, generally using frequency selective a.c. networks, a good example being of course the treble and bass controls on modern Hi-Fi stereograms. But better control over a wider range is possible by voltage-operated circuits. The frequency selective elements of course remain very much as in any other filter configuration, but the control is quite different. This type of circuit is quite old, but in the light of requirements for electronic music composition they have been further developed, notably by R. A. Moog. Unfortunately, to fully exploit their properties requires somewhat complicated circuitry, the most popular arrangement being one consisting of a voltage controlled amplifier with some form of reactive feedback network. It is difficult to obtain uniform results over a wide frequency range with this simple concept and Moog's circuit calls for an adder (but only for multiple input controls), the filter network, an input buffer amplifier and an output buffer stage.

Without exploring the theory of the device, we can say that the cut-off slope is extremely high, possible because the filter proper is relieved of input and output loading by the buffer stages. These, by the way, must be carefully balanced to prevent breakthrough and to prevent the d.c. control voltage from appearing at the output. There are capacitive range switches and an interesting feature is that if the feedback resistor R_f is reduced enough, oscillation takes place; this is in fact a useful source of sine waves of good purity. See Figs. 48–50.

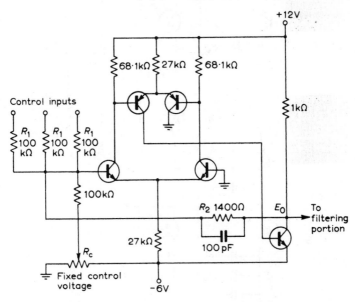

Fig 48   Adder portion of the low pass filter

With slight modifications this circuit can also be used as a high pass filter and by combining the two circuits with a coupling device they can be used as a band pass or band stop filter. If the complete circuitry of Figs. 51 and 52 is used, the centre frequency control shifts the cut-off frequencies of the two filters together so that the ratio between them remains constant;

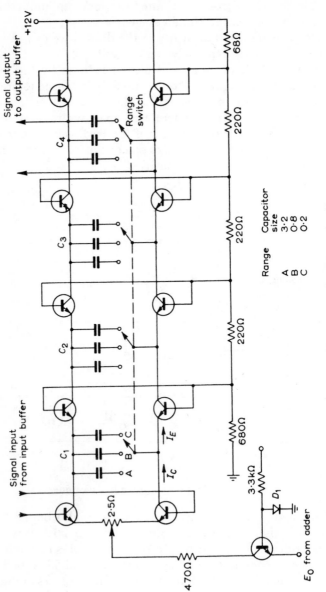

Fig 49   Filtering portion of the low pass filter

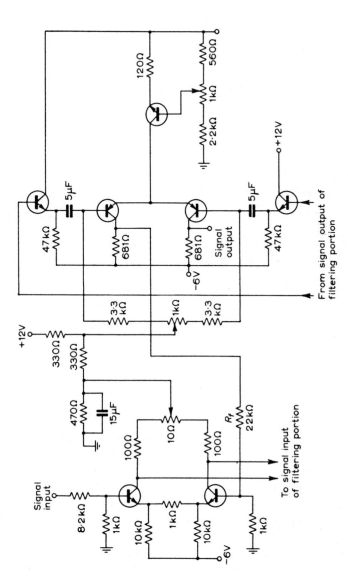

Fig 50 Input buffer and output buffer portion of low-pass filter

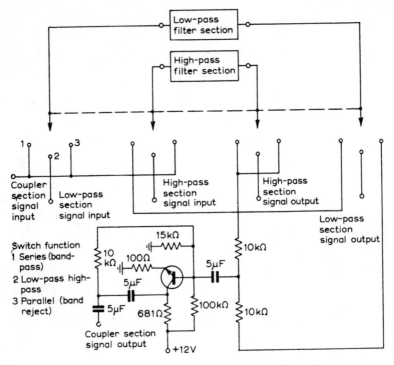

Fig 51   Signal switching portion of coupler section

and with the bandpass width control in operation, a positive control voltage will raise the upper frequency and reduce the lower cutoff frequency. This type of voltage controlled circuit is now in extensive use, and many variants are in existence.

Manual operation of these circuits is quite simple, in general, requiring only a rehearsal or two; but it is as well to work to a known tempo, initiated perhaps by a metronome, and duly noted for future operations. It is also perhaps necessary to make starting or other synchronizing signals on the tape, so that matching up is made possible for further recordings on top of the first ones. Clearly we are touching on the fringe of composing methods here, for the mental process of a composer is divided into two parts—the creative impulse from the imagination, and preoccupation with the method to fulfil the

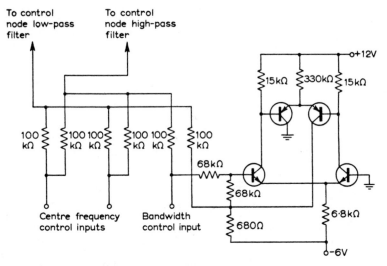

Fig 52   Control voltage processing portion of the coupler section

former. This aspect will be examined a little more closely when composition is briefly touched on.

Now we have seen most of the apparatus for very simple tonal experiments, and with which a great deal of composition can be recorded. But no mention has been made of a noise generator for special effects. This may sound a retrograde step, considering that noise of a circuit nature is something to get rid of, but in fact noise of the proper spectrum and fully controllable can be very useful. After all, the cymbal, side drum, tom tom etc are pure noise and it is possible to modulate noise with tones to produce effects like the well-known one of wind in the telegraph wires, or the Aeolian Harp.

Let us now look at two types of noise generator. The first is a valve unit, Fig. 53, for those who have essentially valve equipped apparatus in any case. The coil is ½" in diameter and has 20 turns of 24 swg enamelled wire on each side of the centre tap. The entire generator including the valve must be inside a screening box. The noise spectrum will have to be shaped by means of previously described apparatus, and restricted as to frequency pass band by some form of filter; as an example, to provide a band suitable for noise of the cymbal type, a 100 millihenry inductor shunted by 470 picofarad should suffice. This would be in shunt across the output from the amplifier following the generator.

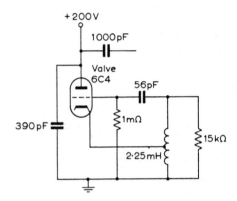

Fig 53   Valve noise generator

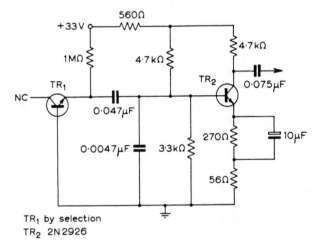

Fig 54   Transistor noise generator

It is more probable that the experimenter would be using solid-state apparatus. In this case, the noise unit can take the form shown in Fig. 54. However, the actual "quality" of the generated noise will depend on the noise from the diode, and it will be necessary to select until the correct effect is obtained.

Noise from one of the diode sections of a transistor is much more random and unsteady than that from a valve oscillator, which after all is really a high frequency fundamental with added harmonics. There is no tuned circuit with the transistor; this is added afterwards to process the resultant wide frequency spread engendered. In this circuit we show an amplifier following the generator; it will be appreciated that instead of the tuned circuit of 100 mh mentioned above, any part of the noise spectrum can be isolated by a suitable tuned circuit. For instance, voltage controlled filters can be used. One important point, however; the applied line voltage must be stabilized in both cases above.

Initiation of the noise signal may be by any convenient method, again very simple contacts (e.g., a microswitch) can be used to start the circuits. One-shot oscillators are useful for lower pitched noises, an example of which is also shown in Fig. 55. Simple experiment here will produce signals of short

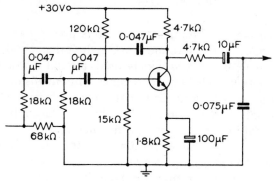

Fig 55   Electronic drum beat oscillator

duration and of many pitches, covering most applications of noise, the main use of which is as a rhythm marker. To this end, we show a circuit for an electronic cymbal in Fig. 56. The synthesis is only moderate and can be greatly improved on, but only by means of more complicated apparatus.

One of the essential ingredients of most music is reverberation which can, in extreme cases, be extended into echo. Remarkable effects have been secured by recording with echo or super-imposing this at a later date. In direct synthesis by whatever means, there can be no effect of this nature, because reverberation is an acoustic phenomenon and is never the same twice for different sounds in different buildings. So the normal calculations to introduce or suppress reverberation do not enter into electronic music techniques. Whilst real acoustic echo chambers

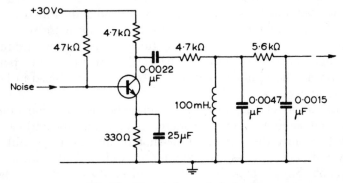

Fig 56   Electronic cymbal circuit

are often used in broadcast work, this presupposes the use of actual sound and microphones. On the other hand, magnetic storage systems are also widely used, though it would be difficult to obtain such long echo times without distortion as one can by using a long acoustic path, e.g., a factory chimney.

Artificial reverberation is usually introduced by magnetic systems employing tape loops or magnetic drums, because there is no real storage time at normal tape speeds, the signal being erased as soon as it has passed through the device. If we look at Fig 57, it will be seen that the signal is fed to a recording head k_1 which is preceded by an erase head k_r. Additional recording heads k_2 to k_6 are spaced out at distances to give successive delays, easily calculated from the known tape speed or rate of drum rotation. Because the head spacing must not be so great as to give the impression of a number of separate signals, the total delay cannot be sufficient for a great many purposes; therefore, a feedback circuit is used as shown in the diagram, whereby some of the output from selected heads is returned and superimposed on the input. This will result in another series of six weaker but further delayed signals in the output, and indeed it is possible to do this once more so that, in fact, if the original delay was 180 milliseconds, the second feedback would extend this to 360 ms, and the final extension would produce 540 ms, which is a good value for many purposes. There is, of course, no reason why signals should not be supplied to a loudspeaker

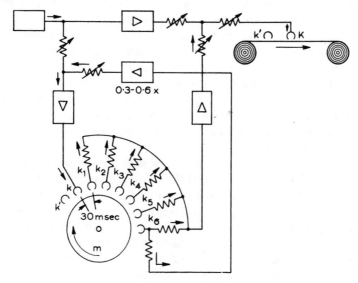

Fig 57   Reverberation by magnetic loop tape

from the music tapes, fed to a long period echo chamber, then picked up by microphones and returned to the tapes.

Mechanically, it is easiest to use a loop of tape, perhaps 3 ft long, of which some 12–18 inches would embrace a brass drum having a very accurately machined face and bearings. Spring loaded rollers hold the tape to the drum face and the heads are lightly in contact when required. The heads are accurately ground to the drum contour, but the ratio of diameters is usually great so the friction is very small. Electrically, there is a limit to the number of feedback paths, since the overall frequency response is not completely flat and this progressively becomes worse. Small magnetic delay machines are commercially available, the only maintenance required being the cleaning of heads and occasional renewal of the tape loop. It is possible, in some designs, to position the heads on the smooth or non-magnetic side of the tape, so preventing oxide pickup on the poles of the head; the increased separation, which results in loss of some high frequencies, can be compensated for either by top note "boost" or by much narrower head pole gaps, since there is now no risk of clogging of the gaps, and a cleaning device can be used to rub on the tape.

Another method of obtaining reverberation is to make use of a transmission line. This is really an electromechanical converter, the signal being applied to a magnetic or crystal driving device which imparts a torsional movement to a coiled wire of considerable length. It is quite possible to calculate any delay, absorption or transmission factor for these wires, but since they are quite easily obtainable on the open market, it is best to purchase as required.

The rate of propagation in a wire is a function of its length and the transmission rate of the material itself; the wire might be straight but is more conveniently in coiled form, to take up less space. The rate of propagation is the same for all frequencies, and if the wire is coiled in a constant-diameter helix, this will be true. But if the diameter of the helix were to vary, the rates of transmission would also vary as the mean length of the turn. In this way it is possible to obtain delays which obey some law in relation to frequency, which is the natural function. On the other hand, multiple springs can be made to produce many phase relationships which produce curious fluttering reverberations because of this constantly changing phase. The music signal is applied to the wire via an amplifier and recovered from the other end by a transducer. It is then either used on its own or combined with the original signal in any desired proportions. The overall design of the system will determine the time in toto, some of the signal being of course reflected a number of times to and fro with continually decreasing energy. A diagram of one method can be seen in Fig. 58. There must always be some means of regulating the energy delivered to the line to prevent overloading, and quite often it is necessary to have filter circuits to limit the frequency range applied; obviously large low-frequency signals would seriously disturb the line. For this kind of work, a conventional

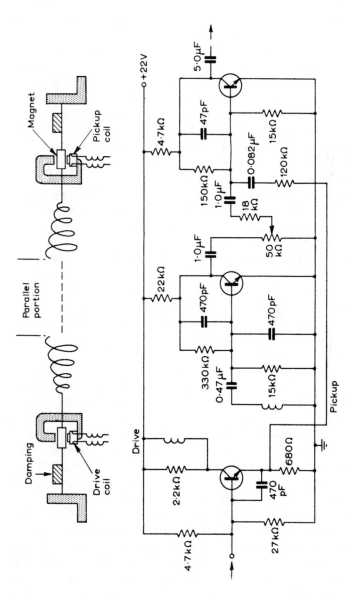

Fig 58 Taper spring reverberator and drive amplifier

echo chamber is much superior. In sounds of such complexity as may exist in electronic music, it is extremely important to avoid any trace of distortion. Other devices are in use, sheets of thin steel with the signal fed in at one corner and taken off at a diagonally opposite corner, and of course the acoustic delay line, in which the signal is supplied by a pressure loudspeaker unit to a long pipe, 100 ft or more, with negligible internal friction. The microphones to pick up the sound (as it must be in this case) are spaced at intervals along the tube to spread out the delay time. Such a system introduces no distortion and is unaffected by external sound or vibrations of any kind.

Having seen the basic elements required for simple synthesis, let us now look at some of the more sophisticated equipment available to perform the most complex intricacies of electronic music construction and composition. It will not take the reader long to see that even the most elaborate machine is only an extension of the simple elements, made more convenient for manipulation by some system of cross-connecting or patching as it is usually known. In some methods, the mechanics predominate, in others, the electronics take precedence. This difference is usually due to the inability or otherwise of the machine to store the processed data before committing it to tape for recording or re-recording.

Then again, one must consider the studio requirements; if it is necessary to have portability, then a smaller device would be favoured; if the studio is a fixture, then there would not be any limit to the weight and possibly the bulk of the apparatus. It could be better laid out and more accessible for servicing. Today, however, thanks to the transistor and allied semiconductors, a complete synthesizer can be made in a surprisingly small container, and in fact the British VCS-3 is only 438 mm high by 444 mm wide by 419 mm deep—a remarkable achievement. Several applications will come to mind. It can be used as a complete unit in itself, using its internal loudspeakers. It can be used as the main unit of an electronic music studio, in association with tape recorders, oscilloscopes and other devices. It is also a live performance instrument, if connected to external power amplifiers and loudspeakers, and thus can not only supply its internally generated sounds, but also and at the same time it can accept inputs from microphones and other sources. Then it could be used as a sound effects generator for plays or theatre work. And lastly, it is an excellent teaching machine, demonstrating all the main acoustic phenomena simply and clearly. Students themselves can operate it, and again, cathode ray tubes or frequency meters, etc, can be externally connected for demonstration.

A synthesizer of this kind must have multiple facilities for the major parameters. Thus we find the VCS fitted with three independent oscillators, voltage controlled, and having more than one output waveform. The first oscillator can deliver 3 volts peak to peak sine wave, and 4 volts peak to peak on the sawtooth waveform. The available frequency range is from 0·6 Hz to 16,750 Hz and the voltage control sensitivity is 0·32 volt per octave. The second oscillator is similar, but delivers square and triangular output waveforms of 4 and 3 volts peak to peak respectively. The third oscillator is a very low frequency unit, delivering the same waveforms of the same amplitudes, but the frequency range is from 0·015 Hz (equal to 65 seconds!) to 500 Hz. All of these are voltage controlled, the great advantage of which is that control can be effected from a distance, often not possible with conventional circuits taken a long way from their association with other components.

One of the most interesting forms of external control is in the form of a keyboard. Although it is possible to use this in a frequency selective sense with semitone intervals, the keys are really provided as a convenient form of switch to voltage control some of the functions of the VCS-3 in a rapid manner. For example, the output from the monophonic generator in the keyboard can be processed in such a way that the amplitude or loudness (as it appears to be) is proportional to the rate at which a key is depressed. In other words, slow legato operation produces a small signal, rapid depression produces a loud sound. This most interesting device allows flexibility in expression in a manner not previously possible. It is a time-amplitude function but in accordance with the circuitry set up by the patch panel, many other sections of the synthesizer can be controlled by the keys, and at a distance if called for.

We have already pointed out the value of a noise generator,

and this unit produces noise covering the entire audio spectrum. Therefore unpitched noise can be added to existing sounds or frequencies from oscillators, or the noise may be passed through filter units which remove some part of the frequency spectrum as required. The application of noise to a low frequency oscillator would result in a kind of chopped sound, whereas at high frequencies the sound is like frying. Innumerable effects are possible by colouring noise either with steady frequencies or with gliding tones. The noise generator on this instrument can be applied to more than one circuit at a time, so that for instance a chord could be modulated in this way. The noise unit is controlled in such a way that rotation of the knob to the left passes the lower frequencies, all are passed in the centre position, whilst only the upper frequencies are allowed through at the right hand end of the travel, i.e., fully clockwise. There is of course a level control. We use level here in the same sense as amplitude or intensity, audibly manifested as loudness.

To make full use of the many sound sources and to regularize the amplitude of signals produced by the VCS, two preamplifiers are on the panel. Both are similar in performance, and can perform other functions. For example, they can process an audio signal brought in from an external source; influence devices in the VCS from an external control source, such as a microphone, a disc or tape player, or another VCS or a remote control, which could be a long way from the apparatus as the preamplifiers are also voltage controlled. For instance, gain can be thus controlled remotely. Of course, the preamplifiers as well as the main amplifiers could be used for any purpose at all, since all inputs and outputs are floating and not connected to the VCS until patched in. They thus become general purpose amplifiers. Since the frequency response of the preamplifiers is uniform for all conditions, there are only gain or level controls; all other characteristics of the sound are engendered by the source controls.

Ring modulators have already been mentioned. The usefulness of this device has not, until very recently, been fully recognized. Some types of circuit distort the waveform and give rise to doubts as to its usefulness; but in the VCS there is a highly efficient circuit with no transformers or diodes, which enables a host of otherwise impossible effects to be obtained. The modulator does not just mix sounds applied, it completely transforms them and the output consists of new sounds which were not heard at all at the inputs. These new sounds are the result of adding and subtracting the input frequencies, giving sum and difference frequencies which only rarely relate harmonically to the original frequencies. By beating two of the internal oscillator frequencies together as shown, then as the variable frequency unit is gradually changed in pitch towards a lower octave, the two sum and difference tones resulting can be heard, one rising in pitch and one falling, as in Table 4. Note that sine waves only must be used for this kind of treatment, complex waves will yield results of a very confusing nature, incapable of analysis. After processing in the modulator, resultant signals can be shaped, filtered, or otherwise manipulated to give endless effects. Because the modulator responds to most frequencies equally, the only control is for the level of the modulated output.

Table 4 Production of sum and difference tones

Falling

Sums	600	580	560	540	520	500	480	460	450	*Heard*
Oscillator 1	300	280	260	240	220	200	180	160	150	*Suppressed*
Oscillator 2	300	300	300	300	300	300	300	300	300	
Difference	0	20	40	60	80	100	120	140	150	*Heard*

Rising

We know that complex tonalities cannot be synthesized without the use of filters, unless the method is that of additive synthesis. By far the most extensive category of sounds are produced by subtractive filtering from complex waveforms. The filter on this instrument has two functions; the actual frequencies to be removed can be selected by a knob, and the sharpness or spread of the filter is controlled by another knob. In other words, the bandwidth is adjustable over a wide range, making the filter sharp cutting or the exact reverse; as the response control is turned to the right, the bandwidth contracts from the low frequency end until the filter has a sharp peak at a frequency determined by the frequency control knob. This circuit is capable of a very high "Q" or selectivity, and at maximum Q it can oscillate. Under this condition, an extremely pure sine wave is generated, which has many uses.

One of the most important components of any music processing system is the envelope shaper, which is responsible for the way a sound starts, the way it behaves during its steady state (if there is one), and the way the sound finishes. The main control exercised, therefore, is one of time. One can see that if for instance a string is plucked, the sound could start almost instantly, not maintain itself, but almost at once begin to die away; though not as rapidly as it began. Or, it could start in a different way, perhaps reversing the times, and hold steady for a period of time; then die off quickly. This is possible with the shaping circuits on this instrument, either as a one time function or as a repeated characteristic which can be set up automatically within the limits of the circuit. Six controls are associated with the shaper, two of which set output levels, the others being timers; attack times from 2 ms to 1 second; on, 0 to 2·5 sec; decay 3 ms to 15 sec; off, which lengthens the automatic off time from 10 ms to about 5 sec. If the full time is used, the circuit will not repeat and must be re-activated by an attack button, fitted on the lower front panel. If this button is pressed, then times set up by the other knobs will be automatically repeated.

In addition, there are two adjustable outputs; the first one is the normal signal output, namely, the injected signal with the desired shape imparted to it. The second output makes this shape available (even in the absence of an input signal) for whatever control purpose may be needed. A lamp indicates the progress of the shaper, it will glow whilst the attack or hold-on time is in use, and become dim or go out during the decay and off time. Clearly it is not possible to describe all the effects possible with the shaper, since there is an endless combinational possibility bearing in mind the cross-connecting of sources and treatments which is possible by the patch panel, q.v.

Reverberation in this machine is supplied by a double spring unit rather like those used in electronic organs, and having similar delay times. There is no provision for echo, which of course is a repetition of the signal one or more times and is quite

different from the prolongation of the sound due to reverberation. In common with the other units on the VCS, the
reverberation circuits are quite independent of any other device,
and are patched in as required. Reverberant sound is most
effective when applied to single stroke sounds, e.g., a bell.
There is a control to vary the amount of reverberation mixed
into applied signals, and one to control the proportion of direct
to reverberated sound. One must bear in mind that all spring
systems are easily overloaded, leading to distortion of the sound.
So the input must be carefully adjusted. Apart from the patching facilities to be described, the reverberation unit can be
voltage controlled from any suitable source, which could be
automatic for instance.

The electronic gear terminates in two identical output
amplifiers, each of 1 watt capacity, and two internal loudspeakers are incorporated although the amplifier outputs may
be taken out to external equipment through sockets provided.
As with all the other panels, these amplifiers are quite independent and can be used as general purpose units. Although
flat in frequency response, a limited degree of tone control is
provided in the output filter panel, which can be used to cut
either treble or bass if required. The amplifier gain controls are
of the voltage type. Muting switches allow one to disconnect the
internal speakers when using other equipment, since it would be
unlikely that other loudspeakers, perhaps of greater power,
would have the same frequency/intensity curve and the resultant
sound would be confusing. Since many of the sound treatments
have the properties of stereo, there is a control to enable the
operator to swing the sound from left to right, which, in conjunction with the reverberation device, enables many spatial
effects to heighten the effect. Lastly, there is a meter on the
upper panel which can perform a great many functions. It is a
centre zero instrument of 1 ma full scale deflection, and can be
patched into any of the voltage operated circuits, and in
addition, can be made to read a.c. or signal frequencies up to a
point, or measure the comparative amplitude of two a.c.
signals. It is even possible to evaluate a waveform by watching
the rate of movement of the needle over a period of time. And
of course it is valuable for fault-finding. A switch changes from

d.c. (control voltages) to a.c. (signal levels). Naturally, only one function at a time can be connected, because if several circuits are simultaneously connected, then this will join the signal circuits, which could produce very misleading results.

The whole of the system described is controlled from a patch panel or matrix board on the sloping lower deck of the synthesizer. This panel is specially designed to overcome the inconven-

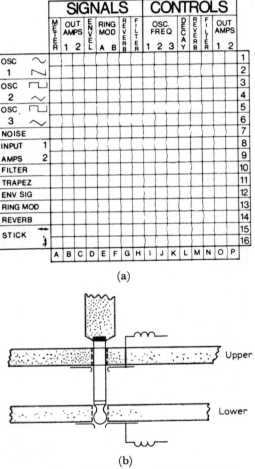

(a)

(b)

Fig 59   (a) Appearance of patch panel. (b) Method of cross-connecting with patch pin. No diodes used

ience of using patch cords, which become entangled one with another and are a nuisance. Moreover they break easily and require a good deal of space for a comprehensive system. Accordingly, this miniature patch board permits of 256 different connections to be made by the simple insertion of small pins. Inserting a pin connects one input to one output, the inputs being arranged in vertical rows clearly identified; whereas the outputs are in horizontal rows, equally well identified. Figure 59 illustrates the matrix system, which is simplicity itself. One must of course remember that no sound can be heard, no matter what is set up, unless the output amplifiers are energized—in other words, there must always be a pin in letter B or C, or both. It is readily seen that the matrix board divides into signal and control sections, and this permits of yet another form of control, the double potentiometer or joystick unit, in the centre of the sloping desk to the right of the matrix board. This joystick can be moved just in the way the name implies, but of course the action is really across or up and down. By regulating voltages obtained from the internal circuitry, it can affect any of the modules which are susceptible to voltage control. To give an example. Connect oscillator 1 to B1 and 2; put a pin in 1·15, which is the left to right movement of the stick. If this latter is now operated, by adjusting the range control the movement can be made to cover any frequency range required; for instance, it could be an octave. If now oscillator 2 is set up in the same manner and patched to the up and down stick, it will be possible to produce any two-part chord within the limits of the ranges set, at some position of the joystick. It is clear then that this device could be used as a vernier on other controls, or to test their setting. But it should be remembered that since it is a d.c. voltage control, it cannot be plugged into any of the signal inputs; on the other hand, several of the control pins could be linked together, in which case all the parameters would be simultaneously altered by the one movement of the stick.

This description is concluded by giving in Figs. 60 and 61 two examples of patching on the VCS-3 to produce certain effects. The markings on the knobs represent the panel markings on the synthesizer. We should explain that the expression

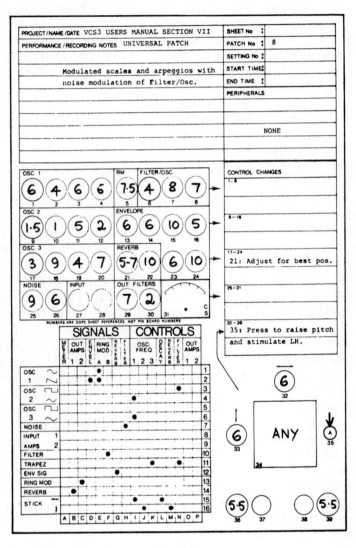

Fig 60   Typical example of VCS-3 patching

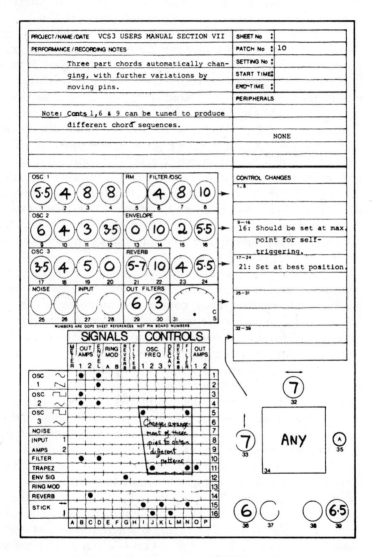

Fig 61   Typical example of VCS-3 patching

"peripheral" means any external control or device connected to the apparatus and not forming an integral part of it.

It will be obvious that the VCS-3 provides the minimum number of sources and treatments for music synthesis or composition; this is reflected in the price, which makes it most attractive for schools and colleges. A new and revolutionary system, far ahead of any other static music machine, is also made by Electronic Music Studios of London. The most interesting features are the built-in digital sequencer, which allows long and elaborate sequences of sounds to be made and edited backwards and forwards on five "tracks." Not only from its own sources, but from any other computer, is it possible to control the computer in this synthesizer. The other feature is that exact measurement of time, pitch and any other parameter can be carried out by the keyboards themselves, thus there are very few controls and it would appear that this instrument will lead the world for some time to come.

Electronically, and unlike any other music system, the EMS control voltage outputs are bipolar, that is, they go both positive and negative. Thus, control and audio signals can be interchanged, and also, the magnitude of a control output can be adjusted without altering the mean level of the parameter controlled. An interesting point is that the noise level from the output is reduced in proportion to the amplifier gain; when this is zero, the noise is immeasurable.

As would be expected, the synthi-100 (Fig. 62) is lavishly equipped with many oscillators, filters, ring modulators and all the necessary equipment for either tape composition or live performance. As with the VCS-3, there are no cumbersome patch cords, but two 60 × 60 way pin patch boards, giving 7200 pin locations. Since there are more facilities than on any other known synthesizer, the pin boards enable rapid and easy control in a small space. However, unquestionably the most interesting part is the 256 event, 6 simultaneous parameter digital sequencer, so a full description is given in Appendix I (p. 125).

We have seen that whatever method is used for setting up musical tones and allied effects, there must always be the basic parameters mentioned earlier. No matter how elaborate the

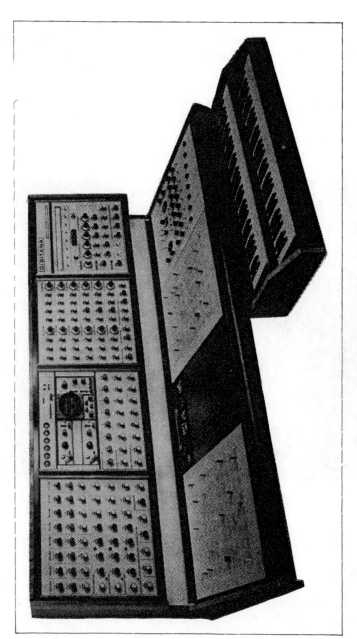

Fig 62 Synthi-100

apparatus, any such complication must be related to ease of manipulation, the production of more than one sound at one time, or facilities for re-recording and mixing and, possibly, the introduction of other pre-recorded sounds from an external source.

In more serious musical studies, it is valuable to be able to keep a copy in "manuscript" form. With some machines, this is not possible, except as a copy tape. With the RCA sound synthesizer (Figs. 63 and 64), however, there is a permanent

Fig 63   RCA Electronic Music Synthesizer Mark II located at Columbia-Princeton Electronic Music Center

record on paper, which at the same time is the master producing the effects. Although a musician with little or no knowledge of electronics can operate this device, it is very desirable to know what the use of the various controls actually does from an electrical aspect; this is analgous to a composer writing for strings without having studied the range of notes possible and the effect of various kinds of bowing, vibrato, etc.

Fig 64   RCA perforator

The initial control of the synthesizer resides in the programming input device, where the properties of the components necessary—frequency, envelope, spectrum, intensity, duration, etc—are specified in the form of binary code instructions, holes punched in a fifteen-inch wide paper roll by keys mounted on a keyboard and arranged in ten vertical columns of four keys each. On the apparatus shown in Fig. 63 there are two complete keyboards, so that two programmes can be simultaneously recorded. The first column of keys represents sixteen binary choices and controls frequency, that is, one element of a frequency class. The second column selects "octave," that is, the position in the tonal spectrum of the frequency chosen. The third column selects envelope, which is the growth, steady-state (if any) and decay characteristics to any desired extent. The fourth column selects the spectrum, or actual tone quality, and the last column selects the intensity.

Those who recall the perforated paper rolls used for the player-piano or pianola will remember that sustained notes were obtained by an elongated slot. The action being pneumatic, this allowed holding up of the striking mechanism or dampers, but with an all electric system where great accuracy is required, slots allow the paper to deform and perhaps tear. Accordingly, an ingenious system of wire brushes above each hole is so arranged that, if a series of holes follows along the same vertical line in close proximity, the contacts made by the brushes do not open until after the last hole is passed. Thus one can sustain a parameter as long as required without slotting the roll.

Pressure on the keys allotted to each section of the roll punches a hole through which the brushes and relays control the output of the frequency generators. There are twelve of these consisting of electrically driven tuning forks tuned to the equal temperament frequencies from 2903 to 3591 Hz. These fixed oscillators are available for any composer who wishes to use equal temperament. There are also twenty-four variable frequency oscillators, tunable from 8130 to 16180 Hz. Any required division of the octave is possible from these circuits, and any octave is possible from the "octaver" section of the roll by suitable punching.

The fixed oscillators have multipliers to raise the useful frequency range. There is also a white noise generator to provide random noise. After passing through the "octavers" the waveform is converted to a sawtooth, which of course means that each original frequency now contains a complete spectrum of harmonic partials (non-tempered of course), in phase, and with the amplitude of each partial related inversely to its numerical position in the spectrum. It is from this sawtooth that the filters of the spectrum section of the roll finalize the tone colour called for.

Passing to the third column of the roll, we have the envelope control. This consists of a series of resistance–capacity networks, whose time constants determine the rate of change of growth (or attack) and decay. Growth times are from 1 millisecond to 2 seconds, and decay times are from 4 milliseconds to 19 seconds. There is an infinite variety of times possible so that the slope of a sound can be made to conform to any law—not necessarily to any law of nature. For example, one could have a sound starting very rapidly, then, before settling down to any steady state, it could be made to slow down or alter its "loudless" curve in any way at all. This a multitude of quite new effects is possible, even from one single tone or frequency, just by altering the envelope. This is just one of the points where the synthesizer scores heavily over conventional instruments, for it would be impossible to change the initiation of the sound on, say, an oboe.

Passing now to the next column of keys, there is the spectrum or timbre section. Here we encounter the vibrato or tremolo unit, high and low pass filters, and the main formant or resonating circuits which can be set up by means of patch cords to give 9^{10} different resonance conditions; there are also attenuators here, patchable to give 6^{10} different attenuation positions. Recalling that the synthesizers provide eight such panels, there are 8 times 15^{10} possible filter settings—surely enough to perform any forseeable operation on a sawtooth waveform! But, added to this, is the facility for adding in noise and the introduction of the vibrato. It can be argued that the value of the tremolo is not so great as coding contrasting intensity values on the keyboard; but when three or four tremolo units, each with differing frequency values are cascaded or combined in re-recording, then the complex periodic result is extremely difficult to approximate by intensity coding and of course different tremolo rates can be applied to different frequency components of a single spectrum, through the many filters.

Once a spectrum has been shaped, the resulting signal is taken to one of sixteen amplifier channels. Here again, there is infinite latitude in relating the loudness of one component to another, although this would normally be fixed by the intensity code punchings.

To code his composition, then, the composer first assigns values to the code number for each component, certainly to the ones he intends to use right away. To do this, switches are provided above the keyboard, in rows of four each parameter. They act on the same relays as the brushes. Thus, the aural effect of the sound set up can be tested before actually committing it to the roll. When he is satisfied, he then punches the roll, and plays it back by hand, cranking it across the brushes. It will be recalled that the brushes only operate relays, so that the speed at which the roll is moved cannot influence the pitch, unlike altering the speed of a tape or disc; therefore the effect can be carefully analysed, and correction is possible to a limited extent. For example, holes not wanted can be stopped off with masking tape, and there may be room to punch further parameter holes if some of the values are not correct. By these means, a sound spectrum or composition can be built up note by note until the composer is satisfied. The motor can then be started and the roll played at the normal speed of four inches per second; the duration of a roll is about five minutes. Of course, this represents a straightforward composition process, but the playback speed may be varied, and the roll could even be run backwards. Disc recording was originally provided, but it has been found more convenient to use a synchronized tape multi-track machine. If, for example, two keyboards were in use at the same time, then at least seven tracks could be independently recorded on this machine. Then, the outputs could be combined and re-recorded another seven times. This now produces 49 series of tones. One more step would give 343 series, which is a very complex tone band. There is, in fact, no limit to the synthesis possibilities of the RCA instrument. An example of tonal synthesis, not possible with physical instruments, might be if we took binary 1 to be C, binary $2 = $ C plus a quarter of a tempered whole tone, binary $3 = $ C plus one eighth of a tempered whole tone, and binary 4 be C plus a tempered whole tone (that is, D). Then, by transposing circuit number 1, these tones would not be transposed in the same ratio but by some permutation of the original pitch class.

We have not so far mentioned the gliding or portamento circuits, which enable continuous transition from one frequency to another, as for example in the trombone. This circuit can be patched in to modify any punched steady tone although this requires that more than one person manipulate the controls. Thus we can see that it is easily possible for a composer to "try out" a new work with quite arbitrary tone colours just to get his succession of notes and harmonies correct, all before making a permanent punched record. The appearance of such a roll is seen in Fig. 65, which shows a phrase of a composition for electronic music and carries the punching

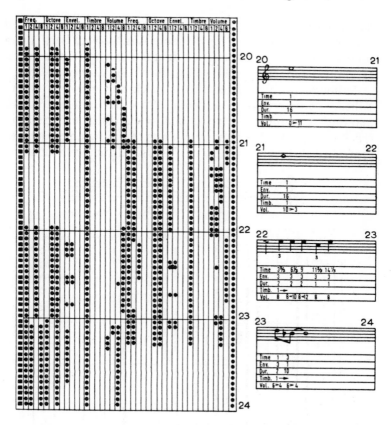

Fig 65 Punched information for RCA Music Synthesizer. Setting-up procedure described on right

instructions to clarify the procedure. In this example, alternate notes are given to left and right channels of the machine. Equivalence with conventional notation is also shown in the drawing. Given a paper speed of four inches per second, sixteen holes per second can pass under the brushes. The normal length for a quarter note is then four holes or one inch in order to play at a metronome speed of 240 quarter notes to the minute. One must be careful to note these speeds, for the tape recorder is synchronously driven by the apparatus, and whilst there can be no alteration in pitch if the keyboard slows down or speeds up, it would be disastrous if the tape speed varied when later the composition was played back on a standard machine. We might add that to ensure synchronization, the tape has sprocket holes for the master recording.

Although the perforated roll is quick and easy for an unskilled operator, certain advantages accrue from continuous marking as in the figure appended, where lines are drawn in reflecting ink, to determine the limits of the parameters to be controlled (Fig. 66). Small exciter lamps and photocells mounted

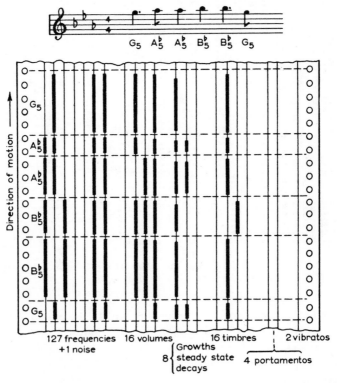

Fig 66   Ink marking for photocell pickup as an alternative to punching

above remove the information and cause relays to operate the respective parameter racks.

We have seen that the RCA machine is a storage device, and another example is the Oramic graphic system. Whereas with

RCA all the parameters are combined on one master perforated control element, in Miss Oram's device all the parameters are individually compiled although mechanically coupled; therefore any one (or more than one) parameter can be removed from the realization at any time and, like RCA, all can be stored after final processing of the sound event.

The idea is very simple; basically there is a series of transparent perforated film strips, all spaced out above a table or platform and all passing over sprockets attached to a common feed and a common takeup shaft. By means of opaque adhesive tape, or by drawing with a felt pen if desired, information is imparted to such strips as may be required. On rotating the shafts, all tracks move together from right to left and pass over photocells which are constantly illuminated. The patterns on the various tracks then modulate the steady light and give rise to corresponding voltage or current changes in the photocell outputs. These changes now control devices which are the basic parameters; oscillators, envelope shapers, intensity and so on. Timbre or waveform is controlled in an ingenious manner. The oscillator waveforms are supplied to cathode ray tubes, the pattern appearing on the screens. A glass plate, carrying an opaque mask of the desired type, is placed over the tube face. The outline of the scanned waveform on the mask is seen by a photomultiplier, which superimposes this signal on the frequency outlets of however many oscillators are being used as pitch sources, for there are several cathode ray scanners. A mask can be instantly removed and changed and herein lies the extreme versatility, because *any* waveshape can be drawn or otherwise applied to the glass plates.

Now since all the functions emanating from the photocells are merely control currents, it does not matter at what rate the tracks are moving—except that analogue tracks such as duration, vibrato and envelope control will have different values. Digital tracks such as timbre, frequency and intensity will not be affected. Therefore having graphically processed one or more tracks, the whole series can be moved across the photocells quite slowly, by a handwheel, to evaluate the resulting sound. Any modification is easily and quickly carried out by stripping off the tape and applying more in any required manner. Note that the tape does not require great accuracy in cutting. The frequency control, for example, must be correctly placed vertically, i.e., as if it were a note written on a conventional music sheet. But the actual size and shape are not important; the envelope shaping track controls the onset of the sound, the intensity track governs the loudness.

Two features of this system which are probably more sensitive and accurate than in any other synthesizer or composing machine are the envelope and vibrato tracks. Because the gradients or rates of change can conform to any contour of the opaque part of the track, very fine nuances are possible. This overcomes the somewhat "mechanical" nature of certain electronically composed music.

To revert to the apparatus proper. The track sprockets for either feed or takeoff are secured to spindles running in accurate bearings. Those on the right draw unused film from the magazines up to the graphic table. Normally there would be three frequency tracks, one envelope shaping track, one intensity track and one vibrato track. Further source controls, e.g., noise colouration or adjustable filters, would require further tracks, a perfectly feasible addition. The frequency tracks each carry several notes arranged in the same order as on a standard music stave. The relative spacing between them must be worked out in association with the usual track speed of 10 cm/sec, which is obtained in a perfectly steady manner from a motor driving through a clutch for easy disengagement. However, no sound could in any case be heard until the duration track operates, for this controls the gating system initiating the sound—the attack circuit. The expression "sound" is used here to simplify description of the signal parameters, though of course the resultant "sound" is a mixture of all the tracks and is not audible until required. It is because of the action of the duration track gate that the accuracy of the front edges of the note patches need not be too great.

A schematic diagram of the synthesis path is shown in Fig. 67, from which it is apparent that the individual tracks are separately recorded as in Fig. 68. This might at first sight appear to call for a very costly recorder, but in fact by striping the same kind of film as is used for the graphic information and running

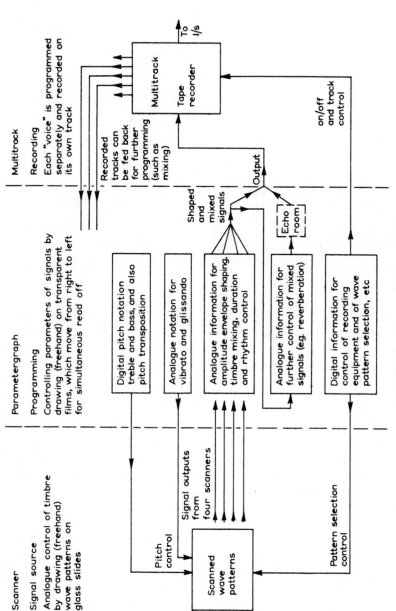

Scanner

Signal source

Analogue control of timbre by drawing (freehand) wave patterns on glass slides

Parametergraph

Programming

Controlling parameters of signals by drawing (freehand) on transparent films, which move from right to left for simultaneous read off

Multitrack

Recording

Each "voice" is programmed separately and recorded on its own track

Recorded tracks can be fed back for further programming (such as mixing)

To l/s

Multitrack

Tape recorder

on/off and track control

Digital pitch notation treble and bass, and also pitch transposition

Analogue notation for vibrato and glissando

Analogue information for amplitude envelope shaping, timbre mixing, duration and rhythm control

Analogue information for further control of mixed signals (eg. reverberation)

Digital information for control of recording equipment and of wave pattern selection, etc

Shaped and mixed signals

Output

Echo room

Pitch control

Signal outputs from four scanners

Pattern selection control

Scanned wave patterns

Fig 67 Oramics graphic sound

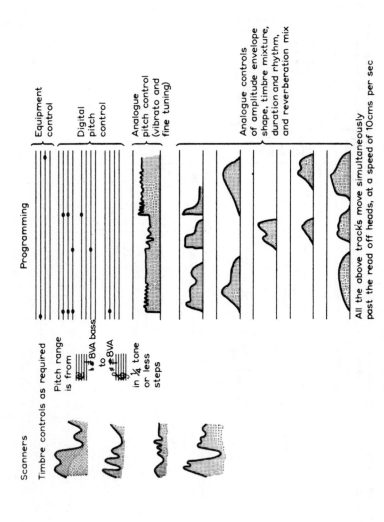

Fig 68   Expansion of Fig 67

this over another set of sprockets geared to the same shafts, synchronous recording must ensue. It is only necessary to provide recording heads and a spring pressure plate, when perfectly satisfactory results can be obtained. Since playback or reading heads are available after the recording heads, either the mixed track signals or any part of them can be heard at once. Clearly any or all of this information could again be mixed into the amplifier input or to ring modulators to give very complex patterns, and of course artificial reverberation is available.

One great advantage of the Oramic system is that the mechanics are relatively simple, being a good engineering project for a university or similar institution, as all the parts can be purchased. If one takes recording facilities into account, this system is probably the least expensive of any, though of course it is not portable like the VCS-3. The teaching facilities are extremely good, especially for harmony and counterpoint, because perfectly conventional methods of composition can be displayed as well as the limitless parameters of electronic music, and with this system any one part of the tonal spectrum can be removed or altered without affecting the remainder. The apparatus is protected by worldwide patents.

Fig 69   Writing and transport parts of Oramic Graphic System

Figure 69 is a photograph of the writing and transport parts of the mechanism, and the reading photocells are to the left inside the light-tight black box, with their photomultipliers beneath. Note signal tracks nearest to the bottle of ink, with control tracks on the upper four strips of film.

4 Electronic music and the composer

It must not be thought that the desire for greater flexibility in the limitations of the musical scale is of recent origin. Musicians for years have been dissatisfied with tonal limitations and we find Busoni and Schönberg, for instance, conceiving the ideas of an infinite tonal spectrum and an infinite tone colour relationship regardless of the method to fulfil it. Of course this is impossible with conventional orchestral instruments. Busoni himself said that "further development is impossible with our present instruments." Nevertheless, Anton Webern did pursue the idea further, merging it with his concept of the proportional series in which both the harmonic and the melodic employ the same interval proportional series so that the consonances no longer depend on arbitrary or statistical factors but on harmonic ratios, i.e., on acoustical structures which conform to the law of the permutation of series, series being defined as an ordered set of parameter values; and serial structures being formed by varying two or more parameters in discrete steps, giving to each of the parameters values taken in order from the series chosen for the parameter in question. The structure is called complete when it contains all possible combinations of parameter values.

Many of Webern's constructions seem like premature electronic fragments. His permutations of sounds lead directly to the question of shaping sounds by the grouping of sinusoidal tones. A sinusoidal tone is in a way, a misnomer; such sounds are pure sine waves and as such, have no "tone." They are the basis of all musical sound processes, but as such are no more than an imagined system of reference from which the composer builds structures in the form of sequences, ratios, series and classes.

But electronic music is not twelve tone music, it embraces an infinitely greater number of combinational possibilities. Accordingly, it is even more atonal than atonal music, but does not share its shock effects. Whilst creating relationships between the elements, it appears atonal or abstract when judged by the standards of traditional harmonies, which again means that the infinite number of tonal subdivisions possible fall strangely on ears attuned to the semitone scale—or even the tenth tone scale. The fact that these seemingly abstract forms are derived from a naturalistic all-tone sound material, constitutes the unique property of electronic music. If indeed the elements of music are a shapeless plastic mass, as suggested by Helmholtz in the preface, then electronic music facilities can join the elemental to the ordered side of sound by reaching into chaos and drawing forth the very foundation plans of music.

The complex tone with harmonic partials is composed of a succession of harmonic partials, each of which is in itself a sinusoid. The "tone" of an instrument is not a tone at all, but a sound which is determined by the frequency components which contribute to the timbre. By electronic means, we can, for the first time, make these components variable.

In the simple tone mixture the frequencies of the partials are not harmonically related to the fundamentals; they cannot be expressed in terms of integral ratios. However, mixtures are still mixtures of sinusoidal tones and hence are not to be confused with chords. They can be turned into musical sound much more readily than instrumental chords. Conventional instrumental musical tone mixtures do not persist—they start, maintain for a time, then decay. By electronic means, steady tone mixtures are easily possible.

Noise has character and to some extent, pitch. "Coloured" noise has musically positional relationship; but white noise, extending over the entire range of audibility has no pitch position. Coloured noise, that is, noise with a tone super-imposed (or the reverse) has many uses in composition.

Now two different sounds given simultaneously produce an interval, more than two, a chord. In conventional music complex tone and interval are clearly distinguishable from one another. In electronic music, however, the tone mixture with its high "binding" level forms a bridge between the two. Sounds and mixtures can be composed electronically, not according to the standard of the natural scheme of things or according to the theories of harmony, but according to a pre-scribed composition arrangement. But, to compose success-fully, a good deal of knowledge of a kind not usually found amongst musicians may be required. This includes familiarity with the operation of the equipment and some knowledge of electro-acoustics, which is quite different from the case where a composer makes himself familiar with the technique of the violin or trumpet, with a view to composing for these instru-ments. Whether he regards any kind of apparatus as his "instrument" now, or whether he considers tape recording as the new technical form of composing, the fact that he is no longer moving in a solidly constructed tonal system places him in a quite new situation. He finds himself able to shape the musical material in his mind to embrace all known and un-known, possible and imaginable sounds; and this of course makes it necessary to think in these new dimensions. Tradition may now be discarded; it is for the musician alone now to decide whether the acoustic material which will evolve from his electronic manipulations shall contain those elements of order which in the traditional sense can be called elements of music. But the basic building blocks can be re-orientated pitchwise to maintain all the timbres with their rich variations, and at the same time to give tremendous dynamic range, tempi and brilliance of figures not subject to human limitations, complete freedom to use and combine any rhythms or accents, unlimited percussions, noise and quasi-musical waveforms, the use, for the first time in music, of the pure sinusoid as a "tone" on its own. And all the other subjective attributes of music.

Clearly what has been said relates to man-made music. It is possible to compose by a machine, and much work has been done on this aspect. But a machine cannot think, and composition is a mental process. If sufficient information is fed to the right kind of machine, an order of probability results which could be interpreted as a form for deriving musical sounds. This indeed has been done, but if the information follows a known pattern then the machine must produce a similar pattern even if it is different in some ways. A machine is well suited to providing a formal structure underlying the composition, indeed it can do little else. This must be considered a limitation, since above all else, electronic systems are completely devoid of form. Therefore a composer must bear in mind that the main basic parameters are frequency, intensity and time. All else derives from these.

As has been said, composing is a mental process and therefore personal and not possible of communication to another except in the form of a realization of that process in sound. It is not possible to lay down any rules of composition, but this must be regarded as a situation which opens up an unparalleled vista of possibilities because of the flexibility of the medium. Suppose one were told that any sound of any kind, within the limits of audibility, could be constructed, and that any number of such sounds could be added, together or serially, in any way for any length of time and with any kind of loudness level or range, would not this tend to inspire a composer to forget convention and to seek means to fulfil his hitherto limited ambitions? Even the most conservative musician can at once point to many orchestral limitations which he would like to see removed. Consider, too, the convenience. Instead of having to write many copies of a score, and obtain the services of the required number of musicians, the composer can do all this himself at the cost only of time and inexpensive materials. Further, he can modify and rewrite any part of his work until perhaps a number of interpretations have been prepared, from which he can select. It is not even possible to detail the incredible flexibility of this art.

The facilities available to the composer will determine how far he can go, but systems which store the composition before committing it to tape are to be preferred, since at any instant the previously constructed sounds can again be played and altered prior to permanent recording. It would be reasonable to re-commend the Oramic system for one without long experience in this artform, because here the information is in the form of adhesive opaque tape and so is easily removed and repositioned. Moreover, what has been synthesized can be immediately played back by hand at any speed, even a crawling speed, to judge the effect. The speed of replay has no effect on the pitch, though clearly the actual speed will affect the senses and so apportion values to the sound. The reader will recall that transparent 35 mm cine film is the basic medium for this device, so that the advantage of sprocket holes can be realized. For any multiple track system, it is essential to have perfect synchronization between tracks, and this is best attainable by perforated material.

The composer must bear in mind that the transfer of the limits of musical composition from the existing limits of the non-electric medium and the human performer to this most extensive and flexible of media imposes its own limits in the form of far less well-understood limits—the perceptual and conceptual capacities of the human auditor. An electronic composition pushed to the limits of the apparatus may cause frustration and bewilderment on account of the radical departure from traditional laws and the production of stimuli to which the auditory system is not accustomed, the most difficult parameter to assimilate being the infinite gradations of the time scale possible, upsetting all concepts of rhythm and tempo (in a traditional sense). This is because of the property of electronic systems to hold a note indefinitely, or to make it so short of duration that it is hardly audible. The composer must get used to the interval controlling and envelope system of the machine he is using.

Let us look at the requirements for a serial sound structure generator. A serial sound structure generator (SSSG) is an electronic system designed to apply serial logic to parameters which characterize musical sounds so that the composer may evaluate the result. It does not produce complete compositions, but in what follows the composer can hear the sound structure at once and modify any part of it at will. We have already explained the meaning of parameter, series, serial structure etc. The maximum variation structure is a complete structure in which no two adjacent parameter values are the same. Such a structure can only exist when for any two series A and B in the group of series, the number of terms in A and the number of terms in B have no common factor. If for example three series have 10, 11 and 12 terms, there is a common factor of 2 between the first and last. This could not be a continuous structure.

Table 5   Notation for one sound event in a serial structure

Parameter A	4	Duration
Parameter B	1	Pitch
Parameter C	3	Intensity
Parameter D	7	Timbre

In Table 5, let four parameters A, B, C, and D be the variables. The numbers in the centre column could be used to describe the sound event and would mean that the A parameter had the value shown by the fourth term in the A series, the B terms had the value given by the first term in the B series, and so on. If the parameters shown on the right side of the block were used, the sound event would have a duration as shown by the fourth term in the duration series, and so on. The simple example of a serial sound structure complete is shown in Fig. 70. Here there are two series, the duration series

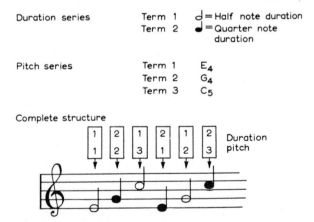

Fig 70   A serial structure formed from two short series

having two terms only; term 1 is a half note duration, term 2 a quarter note duration. The pitch series here has three terms: E4, G4, and C5. The complete structure contains six sound events, because the two series can be associated in six ways. So also it is clear that this is a maximum variation series, because there is no common factor to the number of terms in the two series. The notation used in Fig. 70 as well as the conventional musical notation is shown.

To execute the above, an electronic switching system is required, as in Fig 71. Impulses are transmitted serially between

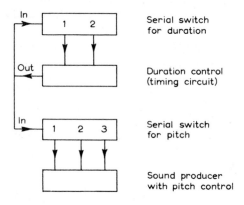

Fig 71   Connection for structure in Fig 70

the parameter switch banks, which have been previously set up to give the independent values of the example. At the end of the process, all is repeated again unless arrested by some means. More complex series structures can of course be set up and explored in the same way, and hybrid structures are also possible, wherein some parameters are controlled by series whilst the remainder are controlled by other means, perhaps manually or by a random system. Of course, the pitch or frequency term in these experiments need not be a single tone, there might be frequency dividers to add octaves or there might be some other interval to the harmonics added, thus a complex chord could be formed for one pitch parameter.

Departing from the question of the mathematics of composition for a moment, consider music as a form of communication. Indeed this must be so, and in this case we can introduce the concept of entropy. Entropy is really the degree of randomness in any system. Where there is a high order of uncertainty, the entropy is high; where there is much similarity or even symmetry, the entropy is low. Melody must then be associated with a state of entropy sufficiently low that a definite pattern is established, yet high enough to have sufficient complexity to provide sophistication. In general, real music has a relatively low value of entropy and that being the case, statistical analysis can be carried out on simple melodies by the same composer; for if these melodies have stood the test of time, and are popular, then such an analysis is valid.

As an example of this approach, a number of Stephen Foster melodies were analysed to ascertain the degree of entropy.* One

Relative frequency of the notes in eleven Stephen Foster songs

Note	B_3	$C_4^\sharp$	D_4	E_4	$F_4^\sharp$	G_4	$G_4^\sharp$	A_4	B_4	$C_5^\sharp$	D_5	E_5
Relative frequency	17	18	58	26	38	23	17	67	42	29	30	17

Fig 72   The notes of the musical scale used in the analysis of Stephen Foster songs

might deduce in advance that there would be considerable similarity, and indeed a first order of approximation shows that twelve notes only are required to compose this type of melody. The frequency of occurrence of these twelve notes is shown in Fig 72, which also gives the twelve notes in question. This in-

* Figures 72, 73, 74, Table 6 and some of the text relating to the Stephen Foster analysis are from *Music, Physics and Engineering*, by H. F. Olson, and reproduced by permission of Dover Publications, New York.

formation is based on eleven compositions, but all transposed to one key, D major, to ensure uniformity. However, if successive notes are chosen so that their probability depends on the preceding note, the structure becomes more complicated. But this is a more useful source of randomness data; see Table 6. In this

Table 6 Two-note sequences of eleven Stephen Foster songs. Probability of following note*

Note	B₃	C#₄	D₄	E₄	F#₄	G₄	G#₄	A₄	B₄	C#₅	D₅	E₅
B₃			16									
C#₄			16									
D₄	1	1	2	5	3	1		1		1	1	
E₄		1	6	3	4			1			1	
F#₄			2	4	5	2		2	1			
G₄					4	3		6	3			
G#₄								16				
A₄		1			5	1	1	4	3		1	
B₄		1			1	1		9	2		2	
C#₅									8		8	
D₅								4	7	3	1	1
E₅								6		10		

* Probability of not following the preceding note expressed in sixteenths

example, the base of the probability was made sixteen because the analysing machine had sixteen channels; otherwise there is no reason for the figure, but it does give a good spread to the values. For instance, the probability of B₃ following D₄ is so high that it is virtually a certainty. From this table, the style of the composer is evident. The analysis can be extended to the probability of three note sequences. It could be further extended, but taking the three note sequence referred to, and assuming there are trinotes ABA, ABB and ABC occurring 7, 14 and 13 times respectively, this makes a total of 34. Thus, there are 7 chances in 34 that A will follow AB; or 3 chances in 16 (expressed in sixteenths) that A will follow AB.

Rhythm can also be analysed in a similar manner because rhythm is a series of impulses repeated to some pattern; therefore an order of probability results—that is, where there is any defined pattern.

It is then possible to design a composing machine based on a random selection of notes determined by a probability based on preceding events. Without going into such a device in detail, it can be pointed out that the basic instrument is a random number generator, which is useful for all forms of musical composition. One way of doing this is to connect four free-running multivibrators to four bistable multivibrators as in Fig 73. MV1 to 4

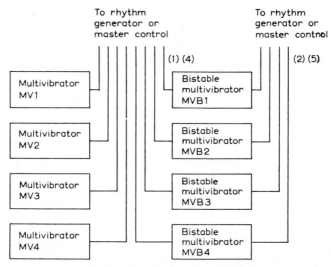

Fig 73   Random number generator

oscillate continuously, and as they feed the bistables B1 to 4, should a multivibrator be disconnected from its bistable, the valves or transistors of this latter unit would remain conductive in one branch of the circuit. If some form of switch connects and disconnects the various multivibrators from their bistables a few times a second, even if this is regularly recurring, the selection of frequencies from the bistables will be random because of the high frequency of the oscillation of the multivibrators compared with the frequency of operation of the switch or controller. Further, as one valve or transistor of the bistable concerned is still conducting on opening the coupling from the drive, there is a standing current available which can be used for operating relays etc. It is clear that if the switch is connected to a random rhythm pattern generator, all forms of probability can be explored. There is no limit to the frequency range of the apparatus, multivibrators are easily tuned and the bistables should be aperiodic and thus will follow any change in injected frequency without adjustment. Of course, a decoding and memory machine could be added as a form of initial control and if this was so, then over a long period of time a definite pattern would result, depending on the information fed to the system, and this would repeat again and again until stopped. Usually the processed signals would be recorded on tape, and this again could be fed in as a control. There is no limit to the combinational powers of a system of this nature, save that there must be restrictions or screening of a mathematical nature applied to the random probability process otherwise the result would be nothing but random and quite meaningless. For instance, even if any musical substance resulted from the electronic operations, the value of the sound could be nil if it had no rhythm or tempo. There are 16 possible quarter-note rhythms in a common time measure alone, coding patterns for this time being shown in Fig 74. These of course are very simple examples.

All of the foregoing methods require that the operator actually manipulates the independent facets of the information, perhaps painstakingly so far as complete assembly is concerned. These means are called tape music, there is nothing against it except that it is very time-consuming. For a complex and complete work, it might mean months of assembly and much cutting and editing of tape. When the art was practised on a very small scale and by few individuals, this was a valid approach.

Now the art of composing electronic music is tending towards methods which can specify the elements for the sound structure with the precision and range of the present-day digital synthesizers. In the forefront of such equipment is the computer, either of an all-digital type or having analogue functions added. This latter must of course be part of the system to introduce the time factor on which the value of the fed-in information in terms of sound depends. Therefore samples of the sound wave to be heard are computed in the form of many numbers which are read out of the computer at a high speed (30,000 numbers per

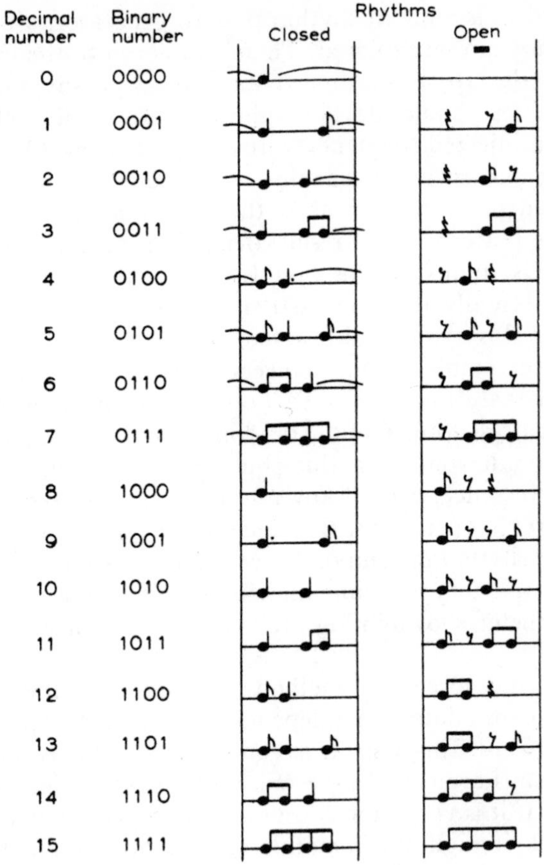

Fig 74   Basic rhythmic scheme for 4/8 meter. (After Hiller and Isaacson)

second to make a sound with a bandwidth of 15 kHz), and supplied to a digital to analogue converter. The output pulses from the converter are smoothed by means of filters and can be heard from a loudspeaker via a suitable amplifying system. It is clear that this process is an extension of the simple analysis given previously. The principles are shown in Fig 75. Of course, the system of providing, say, 30,000 numbers per second would (as such) be too tedious and does not necessarily give the control over the basic parameters which are acceptable. Therefore it is more convenient to programme the synthesis by macro structures called "instruments." These could each be constructed from groups of oscillators, noise generators, etc, and are used as unit instructions. Each unit is controlled by input numbers, being thus the equivalent of the voltage-controlled oscillators and other devices in analogue synthesizers. Being in digital

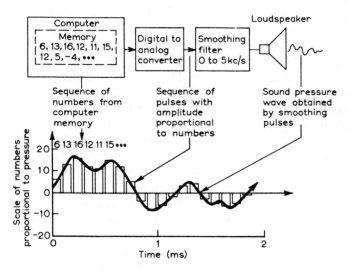

Fig 75   Principle of computer composition. Scale on left is equivalent to loudness

form, there is no restriction on performance speed, but at the same time, without a digital to analogue converter system, there are no nuances or real time adjustment of the sound—it is supplied unalterable from the computer. The hybrid synthesizer solves these problems.

A digital computer is provided with real time inputs which can be played by the musician–performer. A group of digital to analogue converters provide a number of control signals for an analogue synthesizer. Sound from the synthesizer is heard directly by the performer so that he can adjust sound qualities and introduce the amount of performance variation which he wishes. The control signals to the analogue synthesizer are of sufficiently low bandwidth to make a much lower sampling rate from the converter necessary and thus the speed of the computer can be lower; the cost of such a computer can be less than that for all-digital synthesis.

The Frontispiece shows a complete electronic music studio, believed to be the most advanced in the world at the time of writing. From left to right the equipment is as follows. First the teletype perforator for the fast computer type PDP8L, known in this system as Leo and at the top of the first large instrument rack. Beneath the computer are the fast tape reader and digital clock which delivers synchronizing pulses at 400 Hz or a sub-multiple of this frequency. The resulting resolution of 2·5 ms has been found adequate for music realization in this studio. Below the clock are 252 oscillators and a bank of 64 filters, at semitone intervals. Beneath this again is the magnetic tape unit, the fast tape punch, and the disc storage unit. The other racks contain the second computer. Sofka, somewhat slower than the PDP8L, with its perforator (left centre) and the remarkable patch panel which dispenses with cords and enables the whole system to be controlled from this small area in conjunction with the pushbutton panel. Over-riding controls can be seen in the shape of the sixteen pot knobs and there are of course special facilities for audio purposes. The computers control the pitch, tuning, amplitude, waveform and envelope of the seven octaves of oscillators; the "Q", gain and response mode of the 64 narrow bandpass filters covering $5\frac{1}{2}$ octaves for spectrum analysis and synthesis; nine other oscillators and function generators; six amplifiers; two variable response filters; and a number of other devices such as percussion simulators, noise generators for both white and coloured noise, and reverberation units. The extensive patching panel is the main method of setting up the parameter contexts, but up to twenty parameters can be changed during performance by computer-controlled audio switches.

Mixed composite signals can be monitored on the oscilloscope and also through amplifiers and loudspeakers. A four track and four two-track recorders may be used for recording compositions on magnetic tape, but it is one of the great advantages of the studio that it is not necessary to use tape at all until the piece is known to be correct in every detail. Of course, with the storage system the data can be recalled again and again until the composer is satisfied with his realization.

The whole system is called MUSYS and it has two important programming functions. The compiler translates the composer's programme into a data set stored on the disc, and the Performance programme sends items from this data set to the audio devices at appropriate times controlled by the crystal clock. See Fig. 76. Eight independent lists of data may be stored by the compiler, each with its own time scale, so the composer is spared the intricacies of temporal relationships between parts. There is a macro facility which, as has been explained, allows the composer to give a name to a sound or structural element, leaving "gaps" which can be filled by parameters when the macro is called. It also allows sections to be repeated or compiled conditionally as a musical requirement. Either before or during performance, the composer can make use of a control device called the button panel, from which he can monitor, alter and control data going to any of the MUSYS devices; he can also stop, start and adjust the rate of delivery during a performance, and can "single-shot" the delivery routines by turning a knob which the computer recognizes as a substitute for the clock. An editing programme run in conjunction with the button panel enables the data stored on the disc to be altered, providing a way to make fine adjustments which are hard to programme.

Computers use a standard language usually based on the FORTRAN syntax, but of course with such a complex system and if one includes the extensive use of macro facilities, and the fact that the MUSYS system has no Boolean facilities, there must be certain departures from any conventional codes. The operators for MUSYS are—

+ addition	& logical "and" (used arithmetically)
− subtraction	> maximum (e.g., $4 > 7$ has the value &)
* multiplication	< minimum
/ division	

The character ↑ randomizes the expression preceding it; so that, for example, N↑ is a rectangularly distributed random

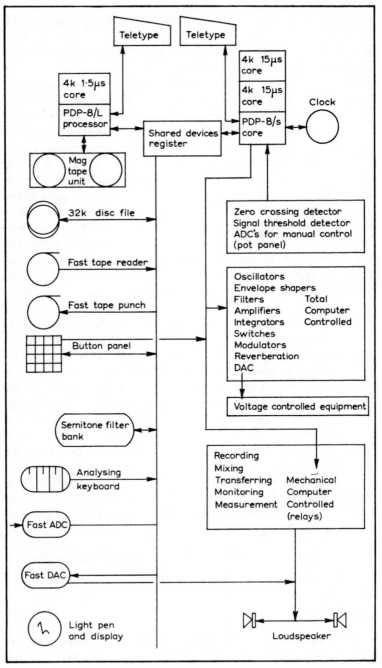

Fig 76   Arrangement of MUSYS apparatus

variable in the range, 1, 2, . . . , N. The character "←" means "read a decimal number from paper tape," and is used for presenting large quantities of data to an MUSYS programme. Data is stored by "." (for six bits) and ":" (for 12 bits). For example, A5.12 "send data 12 to amplifier 5." "n!" selects the data list ($n = 0, 1, . . . , 7$) on which this will be stored. Macros are called whenever ♯ appears. Using parameters they provide the procedural basis for the language. A macro call has the format ♯ *macro name, parameter, parameter* . . . . The corresponding definition has the format *macro name defining string* @. Formal parameters (the gaps mentioned above) appear in the *defining string* as %A, %B etc, where the letter indicates which parameter is to be used. Many other expressions are employed, but the foregoing will give an indication of the design employed.

There is an automatic error detection system, and if the compiler discovers an error in the source text, it terminates the compilation and types an error report, firstly ringing the typewriter bell. There are a number of circumstances when the error codes will be invoked, some of the obvious ones being: no more storage disc space; non-existent list item; parameter number zero or negative. Naturally the setting up procedure will be totally different for different computer assemblies, but since the MUSYS system appears to be one of the most useful synthesizers in existence, we have given in Appendix II short instructions indicating the kind of information required to programme the apparatus, and a part of a composition programme as actually fed to the machine.

It is evident that if the composer can master the language for using the system, then he is relieved of all physical contact with such things as knobs, levers etc which are at first difficult to get used to. In this respect, the computer scores over manually manipulated systems and of course it is far quicker—if time is important. All the same, to digest and punch up the full data does take time; it is only the actual operation of the circuits which is speedy. The computer has the facility to repeat the data again and again if need be, whereas some other methods do not have storage means.

In contrast to the sophisticated MUSYS system, an alternative approach has been used at Toronto in order to save computer time. It will be understood that if the composing system is, let us say, in a university, then a number of music students may well be waiting to use it. Further, it is not improbable that original ideas may be lost if contained only in the head, should the waiting time be excessive. At best there must be frustration. Therefore instead of asking the computer to set up the whole of the waveforms, it can be made to generate voltages which control the instantaneous values of various parameters of the sound waveform, the actual waves themselves being generated by external apparatus. This method only requires a low bandwidth between the computer and the auxiliary equipment, and this allows real time operation with a quite small computer. Since however the control voltages are an indirect form of parameter control, drift and departure from exact frequency etc. might occur in the external equipment; therefore occasional checking and possibly recalibration is required.

The system comprises a computer and a digital to analogue converter. The converter consists of a number of digital potentiometers which can be set in discrete steps, and which control oscillators by voltage increments. However, the pots are linear so an exponential converter changes the slope of the control voltage to approximate more to the logarithmic response of the ear. On the other hand, the gain controls of the voltage controlled amplifiers can be altered linearly or exponentially as required. Since there is a separate amplifier for each of the four oscillators simultaneously controlled, there is no risk of intermodulation. As is customary in methods involving direct current control, a push-pull or balanced amplifier is required to ensure there is no trace of the control signal in the output. Because the control originates in stepped potentiometers, there is a jump (however small) between increments of control voltage; this must be removed before it causes a jump in frequency, so following the pots are low pass filters which act as smoothing devices. There is a fixed time constant for these filters, so that the four processed signals will be in synchronism. It is 20 milliseconds, a good compromise between apparently instantaneous sound and the removal of transients. The computer timing can also be provided by a 40 Hz generator. The arrangement of this apparatus is as in Fig. 77.

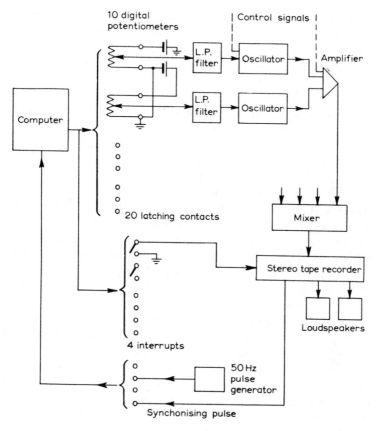

Fig 77   Simple hybrid composing system

Although there is a great simplification of the information supplied to this computer as compared with the MUSYS system, the same basic parameters must always be called up because all music processing depends on the essentials outlined many times: pitch or frequency, duration or envelope, intensity or loudness; and timbre and vibrato as second order ingredients. The combination of some or all of these basic parameters into "instruments" can be used to simplify the language for the computer, so that a wide range of possible characteristics can be controlled from a few input codes. Of course, as in all other systems, an over-riding manual facility is provided although modifications can be made by computer-operated switches if the information is correctly supplied. It will be seen from Fig. 76 that there is a manual mixer for the processed tones, which results in real time control.

As already mentioned, calibration and checking of the voltage-operated external sources may be required from time to time; the more voices combined at one time, the greater the need for accuracy. The computer can carry out instructions to ensure correct setting of the voltage pots, if suitably programmed. So from the foregoing it can be seen that for very precise specification of waveform etc, a digital sampling technique is the best method; but using this kind of hybrid technique, sound compositions, especially those of an instrumental nature, can be accurately and economically programmed. Clearly the cost is reduced and certainly the saving in time (at the actual instrument) is very real. As with any punched information system, the preparatory setting up time away from the machine may be considerable, and this does not prevent the computer from being used by those already prepared.

Now if the composer is a conventional musician trained in the conventional methods of writing and scoring, then if he is going to pursue electronic composition, it is almost certain that he will have to undergo a course of training quite foreign to his conception of sound structures as exemplified by orchestral instruments. In fact, he must start learning a new language relating to electronics, electro-acoustics and to some extent, mathematics. It is perhaps for these reasons that the whole art of electronic music appears to attract more young composers than experienced ones. For example, a composer should understand the terminology of electronics, the ease or otherwise with which he will handle this kind of equipment relating to the degree of understanding of the basic principles. This will be aided if he shows natural curiosity as to how it works. Then, he must understand audio-acoustics. Although such a study is really fundamental to most music, training is rarely given, but even with conventional instruments the use of microphones and loudspeakers is commonplace. It would be as well to have some mathematical knowledge and, if possible, to understand the arithmetic of computers and one of the common computer languages such as ALGOL or FORTRAN. However, even an understanding of the basic rules will help them to converse with computers.

It might be as well for the composer to examine the history of experimental music techniques. There are many equally valid ways of expressing the parameters of music beyond his own, and of course this leads to an examination of other media and their importance for music and art in general. Then there have been many articles, papers and books published over the past twenty years on "new" music theories and their application to the electronic medium. One may ask, where is this kind of training to be obtained? Well, in actual fact it is the electronic music studio which is the classroom and the electronic compositions produced in these studios are the text, for each and every one so far has been an experiment and no two are ever alike. It is an experimental art allied to long proven apparatus such as audio amplifiers, tape recorders and loudspeakers; they are the medium instead of orchestral players, and this leads one to consider the methods of presentation of electrically realized sound.

All such sounds can be heard only through the medium of loudspeakers. Customarily, it has been necessary to separate the performers from the listeners by some spatial relationship, usually in the form of a stage and an auditorium. In a concert hall, the sheer mass of the number of performers makes this essential. Moreover, since there is no control over the type, loudness or quality of the sound beyond that imposed by the conductor and the number of instruments, the total effect is made or marred by the physical construction of the auditorium, manifested as an acoustic phenomenon. The reverberation constant of any given building can only be modified in some rather cumbersome way by alterations of the ratio of reflected to absorbed sound, usually executed by moveable panels or reflectors. The conventional geometry tends to an audience face to face with performers.

If one considers recorded music instead of live music, then quite a casual study elicits the fact that new methods have been evolved for dealing with architectural acoustics whilst recording.

The placing of microphones, artificial reverberation, stereo techniques, amplification procedures within specific frequency ranges and other techniques allow kinds and degrees of definition, balance and general transparency unknown in live music. Recording technique goes beyond traditional three-dimensional architectural acoustics and establishes its own frame of spatial reference, which can be manipulated by the recording engineers in a great many ways. We can of course learn from the cinema to some extent. Whereas at the intro-duction of sound films there were inadequate loudspeakers inadequately placed, things have advanced with multi-track recordings to the extent that, whilst the main loudspeakers are still behind the screen (because the interest lies there), sub-sidiary units can be found in other parts of the auditorium. These may not be in use all the time, but the effect of being *immersed* in a sound field creats a quite new sensation in music and this is something which must be considered in conjunction with electronic music. Since live performances to date have been few and the exploitation techniques are uncertain, little experience has been forthcoming in the placement of loud-speakers for this specialized purpose. But it is reasonable to imagine sufficient numbers of loudspeakers to enable the com-poser to project his spatial ideas in the most effective manner. Intimacy is enjoyed at home with stereo record players, where one is to some extent immersed in the sound. There is no doubt in the author's mind that this is the technique for public per-formance. Multiple loudspeakers do not necessarily mean a very loud sound; rather they mean a total sound field, abolishing the point source effect. To take an analogy, if one enters a church when the organ is playing, the bass pedal notes seem to have no position in the building; they are all-pervading and one cannot pin-point their source. This is because of the long wavelength of the very low frequencies, tending to diffract or creep along the walls, whilst there may be reverberation to heighten the effect; but it is very real. And of course it is well known that the higher the frequency, the more the beam of sound tends to become a point source—certainly with con-ventional cone speakers. Therefore considerable thought should be given to the relationship between audience and loudspeakers in presenting electronic music. This of course tends to other techniques, the illusion of distance, for instance, by sweeping the sound from one unit to others, making it come nearer or further away from the audience. There is tremendous scope for experiment and research in this field, if only to destroy the dimensional impression inherent in the existing architectural characteristics of established concert halls. One must remember that these concert halls were built because at the time this was the only way to bring the public into contact with good music; there was no radio, no records. This phase may take its place with other milestones in history, we do not know yet; it is to some extent bound up with sociology.

In the final analysis it must be recognized that hearing is a very individual thing; no two people hear in the same way. Sometimes it is too refined, sometimes perhaps too coarse, but in any event conditioned by education and long usage. It is fortunate indeed that there is more agreement than disagreement over the character and effect of sound spectra, and this statement is made only to underline that the precision of which electronic composing systems are capable may in fact be too precise for some ears, and to suggest that the user of sophisticated apparatus should exercise patience until he is quite sure of the relationship between the calculated parameters and the effect as heard aurally.

It will be evident to everyone that the tape recorder makes the whole art of serious electronic music possible. It may be asked why, and this is easy to answer at this time. Firstly, sound of any nature impressed on magnetic tape can be monitored, played back, reversed, edited, altered in speed (resulting in pitch changes); other sounds or signals can be superimposed and there is little limit to the number of times that re-recording is possible. Secondly, an elementary form of machine enables a musician to experiment at home and at little cost, the only difficulty being a possible lack of synchronism between material impressed at various times. One of the most important reasons why this facility of re-recording is so necessary is that equipment currently available for musical composition or synthesis is limited as to the number of channels available. Both the cost and the difficulty of manipulation would enormously increase if complete compositions representing many parts could be constructed at once. The general practice is to compose one or two parts, then re-record another two and so on, until the desired effect is obtained. Two has been found the optimum number of simultaneous channels for convenient operation.

It must not be overlooked that some of the sounds on a multiple tape may not be electronic in origin. One can superimpose sounds made by the voice, mouth and lips, and many other actual sounds or noises. This is one way of correcting or adding to a composition which appears to be deficient in some way. The method is made use of in live electronic music performances.

It is clear then that any serious experiments (for every new composition is virtually an experiment) must call for tape recording, and this at once leads to commercial difficulties. Why? Because the linear speed and the position of any part of the tape must be known with accuracy, and it must be possible to revert to any section of the tape within a few thousandths of an inch. This would not be possible without a synchronous driving system, and the most convenient device is tape with sprocket holes or perforations. Of course, this does not mean that standard tape is of no use, a great deal of useful exploratory work can be done with two or three ordinary tape recorders started at the same instant and impulsed with a synchronizing mark—an audible pip, or a combination of these in the form of a code. Some excellent work has been done on simple apparatus of this kind. Recorders used for this purpose should have a monitoring head so that the sounds may be heard all the time from the actual tape itself. Most commercial tape recorders are driven by small a.c. motors of little power; unfortunately, there is no standardization in design, and we find machines with one, two or three motors. This is a defect from our point of view, since it will not be possible to obtain variable speed control. In any case, it is doubtful if the actual constancy of speed (as distinct from the irregularity of rotational speed, generally called "wow") is sufficiently accurate for sine wave processing, for it is an interesting fact that with complex waves small control movements, such as, for example, the steps between one turn of wire on a rheostat and the next, are not observed, whereas with a pure sine wave the difference in level is noticeable. Therefore the control of speed must be carried out by a more complex system, often involving servo methods where an error voltage (derived from the armature) is compared with a controlled voltage, and automatically caused to bring the speed to some assigned figure. Means are provided to alter the control voltage at will and in a stepless fashion to change the rotational speed of the tape drive system as may be required. Alternatively, the speed control may be effected by electromagnetic clutches, impulsed by automatic or manual means, and such clutches can be made very rapid in action—a few milliseconds at worst. Again, variable speed can be secured by a system of cone pulleys, which are stepless, and this is a mechanical method of considerable accuracy, especially useful over wide pitch changes, i.e., an octave or more. Clutches can operate the cones, so that, if suitable cueing or control signal are available, the recorder can stop after every note or structure has been recorded, and wait while the next tone is being set up, when another cue signal will instantly start the tape again. This is economical in tape, though it may mean a certain amount of editing later. Time, however, is one of the factors which cannot be taken into account in this art. It is naturally more economical to use a multi-track recorder if possible, for with sprocket hole tape all the channels can be ferried backwards and forwards until signals are impressed as desired, whether the method is to use many heads on one tape or separate heads on separate tapes coupled by sprockets on a common shaft. The latter arrangement makes it much easier to erase any part of one track without affecting adjacent ones. It is seen that a variable speed recorder of great accuracy is highly desirable and quite essential for some work. All the same, as already stated, some excellent work can be done on ordinary high-quality domestic recorders if suitable cueing methods are devised; of course, two tracks can be recorded at one time on a stereo machine.

In the case of computer composed music, if the studio is sufficiently complex there is no reason why a succession of chords or other complete synthesis cannot be stored and called up when required to impress on a precision recording machine using unperforated tape, provided that it has multiple heads.

The main reason for specialized recorders is to ensure absolutely constant speed; not only is this desirable from a performance aspect, but if the tape holds synchronizing marks on one track or is to be fed back again into the system for re-processing, then the slightest flutter or wow might ruin an expensive composition. Where the utmost precision is called for, the frequency required for the stated motor speed can be generated by a high power electronic oscillator, when it will have a much greater accuracy than if obtained from the public service mains.

Appendix 1

Specification for the Synthi-100

The Synthi-100 is designed for computer interface, and therefore all control inputs are available for direct connection to digital/analog converters on multiway connectors. The overall size base of the "DIGITANA" is 79 in. length by $37\frac{1}{2}$ in. depth, the height is 33 in. and the height from the underside to the ground is 30 in.

SIGNAL LEVELS

The levels of all signal outputs available at the patchboard are controlled by panel mounted potentiometers. In fact, these potentiometers provide control voltages which operate on voltage controlled amplifiers. The advantages of this system include:

Constant low output impedance
No "fader scratch" as levels are changed
Less conveying of signals at high impedance (where they are susceptible to crosstalk)
Much simplified wiring system
Ideal logarithmic control of level
In general, signal levels are about ± 1 Vp–p, although most

Note: This specification is reproduced by courtesy of Electronic Music Studios (London) Ltd, London.

outputs can deliver much more than this. Most devices which have signal inputs are adjusted for optimum operation at this level, although it can be usually considerably exceeded without serious distortion.

INPUT IMPEDANCES

All input impedances are approximately 10 KOHM. This comparatively high figure was chosen as a compromise between the conflicting requirements of "fan out" (i.e., the number of inputs an output may drive before it runs out of power) and susceptibility to crosstalk when an input is left open circuit. Screened cable is used for all signal paths in the studio, and impedance at certain central inputs is made infinitely low so that secondary control parameters can be added without re-adjusting the magnitude of the primary ones.

A *Three voltage controlled audio waveform generators, sine and ramp*

Manual frequency range:	Greater than 1 Hz – 10 KHz (extendible by voltage controls in both directions to 0·25 Hz and 20 KHz).
Sine purity:	Better than 5% total distortion between 10 Hz and 10 KHz.
Ramp output linearity:	Departure from linearity ±1% of best straight line between 10 Hz and 10 KHz.
Voltage control:	0·5 V/octave. Accuracy 0·3% departure from best straight line between 100 and 2000 KHz.
Frequency stability:	Generally better than 2% from month to month, but the oscillators usually hold their setting to within 2 cycles in a thousand during a working session.

A sine shaper control is included by which variable amounts of even harmonic distortion may be added.

B *Three voltage controlled audio waveform generators, triangle and square*

These can be varied from triangle to sawtooth ramp, and from symmetrical square to short pulse, in either polarity.

Manual frequency range: Greater than 1 Hz to 10 KHz.
Triangle symmetry: $\pm 5\%$ rise time to fall time equality.

Other specifications as for sine/ramp oscillator.

C *Three voltage controlled low frequency waveform generators*

Same details as before, but oscillators are twenty times as slow.

Frequency range: Greater than 0·025 Hz (40 secs per cycle) to 500 Hz.
Voltage control: 0·5 V/octave.

These three oscillators are intended mainly as control sources, but can be used for tone generation at the upper end of the range.

All nine of the above oscillators have synchronization inputs so that they can operate at an integral multiple of another oscillator, providing a huge variety of waveforms which can be used in additive synthesis.

D *Three noise generators*

Variable from white (central position of colouration control) to dark or light positions (low or high pass filters).

Distortion: In white position, frequency content is flat ± 3 dB from 100 Hz – 10 KHz.

We recommend several noise sources, because with different filterings more than one can be used for different purposes.

E *Dual output random control voltage source*

This device produces two control voltages which move abruptly from one level to another. The distribution of levels is rectangular rather than Gaussian, and the two outputs are uncorrelated in level, but synchronous in time. The mean time between changes, and the variance about that mean are manually controllable. The distribution of times is rectangular, and in common with all other time control devices in the studio, a control range of at least 1000:1 is available.

Controls:

Amplitude variance:	Up to 2·5 V symmetrically positive and negative (×2, each output separately controllable).
Time range:	From approximately 10 secs to 10 ms if no time variance is applied.
Time variance:	From equal steps to 1000:1 variance. Effect of variance control is obviously limited when time range control is at either entrance.

F *Three voltage controlled trapezoid generators with integral envelope shapers*

These devices might be described as voltage programmeable four segment curve synthesizers, the output being available as two control voltages and as the modulation of an audio signal. The basic waveform produced (at each control output) has four stages:

1 *Delay* The output remains constant and negative for a controllable time after the generator is triggered.

2 *Attack* The output rises to a fixed positive value at a controlled rate.

3 *On* The output remains constant and positive for a controllable time after the completion of "attack."

4 *Decay* The output falls at a controlled rate to its initial value.

In addition, there is a second output which lags behind the first by one quarter of a complete trapezoid cycle. Thus the time set for, say, "on" in respect of output 1, becomes the time for "attack" from output 2, and so on.

The amplitude and polarity of both outputs may be adjusted independently so that if they are summed (on the patchboard) any continuous four line function which ends at the value at which it starts may be produced. This arrangement gives an extraordinarily flexible range of envelopes.

The envelope shaper portion consists of a logarithmic voltage controlled amplifier permanently connected to one of the trapezoids.

The overall control of each cycle of operation may be in a number of ways selected by a switch, having the following positions:

1 *Signal threshold*   Any signal above a certain level initiates a single cycle.

2 *Hold* sequence starts when control is positive. Decay does not start until control goes negative.

3 *Single shot* positive zero crossing initiates a single cycle.

4 *Free run*

5 *Gated free run* positive level allows the sequence to free run. Sequence stops at the end of a cycle, when level goes negative.

PANEL CONTROLS

Initial delay time	2 ms to 20 sec.
Attack time	2 ms to 20 sec.
On time	2 ms to 20 sec.
Decay time	2 ms to 20 sec.

(these parameters may also be voltage controlled over their entire range.)

Trapezoid phase 1 output level (centre zero knob)
Trapezoid phase 2 output level (centre zero knob)
Signal level control
Push button (to initiate cycle)
Trigger mode selector switch

Envelope shaper is logarithmic to within 3 dB over its 60 dB range.

Voltage control function of time parameters is ideally exponential to within 10% (of dependent parameter) over a range of 1000:1. Departure from ideal is gradual beyond these limits. This permits a single voltage applied to all inputs to compress the time scale.

G   *Four voltage controlled filter/oscillators (low pass to resonating)*

Operation as a sine source.

Frequency range:	Greater than 5 Hz–20 KHz.
Sine purity:	Better than 3% total distortion between 10 Hz and 10 KHz.
General noise figure for oscillators:	Spurious outputs not greater than 0·1%.

As filters, they are adjustable from Low Pass to resonating filters, covering the entire sonic range.

Frequency range:	Greater than 5 Hz to 20 KHz.
Low pass position:	Cut off rate 12 dB for first octave and 18 dB per octave thereafter.
Resonator position:	Maximum stable "Q" factor — 20.
Accuracy of exponential voltage Control function:	±1% between 100 Hz and 2000 Hz.

Note: operation as a voltage controlled oscillator is limited by the time taken to respond to an abrupt change. Maximum slew rate is about 2 ms per octave.

H   *Four voltage controlled filter/oscillators (high pass to resonating)*

Similar, but complementary to low pass filters.

I   *One octave filter bank*

This consists of eight resonating filters, fixed-tune one octave apart, in the range 62·5 Hz – 8 KHz, separately controllable.

J   *Two voltage controlled reverberation units*

Each spring unit has two elements with delays of 35 and 40 ms.

Maximum reverberation time:	2·4 seconds.
Useful frequency range.	30 Hz – 12 KHz.
Voltage control range:	±2 v from no reverberation to maximum reverberation.

K   *Three voltage controlled slew limiters*

This device is a unity gain amplifier in which the output exactly follows the input at a rate whose maximum (slew) is defined by a control voltage. One application might be to interpose the device between the pitch control voltage from a keyboard and the oscillator whose pitch is to be controlled. If the key velocity voltage were then applied to the slew control input, the player could produce a glissando between any two notes that he played, the rate of glissando being controlled by his touch.

Steady state gain: $1 \pm 1\%$
Steady state linearity: $\pm 0{\cdot}05\%$ (BSL)
Range of slew control: 1 ms to 10 sec.
Voltage control of slew is exponential.

Note: Unlike all other devices, no output level control is provided as the device has unity gain.

L   *Three integrated circuit transformerless ring modulators*

These very efficient modulators also include amplifiers, and can therefore be used in series for double or triple modulation.

Maximum input for
undistorted output: 1·5 V p–p to each input.
Breakthrough with 1·5 V on
one input only: 5 mV p–p (-60 dB)

M   *One 256 event, 6 simultaneous parameter digital sequencer*

This machine is, in fact, a small special purpose digital computer, complete with analog to digital and digital to analog converters. It provides a sequence of control voltages which may be used on any of the devices in the studio.

The operation of the sequencer may most easily be described in terms of conventional music, although it must be remembered that the design by no means limits it to this kind of operation. The sequencer stores 256 "notes" and plays each note at the correct time and for the correct duration. It simultaneously provides two voltages, one of which might be used to define pitch and the other loudness. It is capable of controlling three voices, each with duration, pitch and loudness. The 256 note storage may be distributed to each voice in any proportion, for instance, 254 notes may go to one voice and one each to the others. In fact, the second and third voices need not be used as such, their voltages could be used to control parameters (filtering, decay time, etc.) of the first voice.

The information which is to be stored and subsequently reproduced is presented to the machine as control voltages, which are most easily supplied from the keyboards.

All timing data are entered by playing the keys. To record a sequence the composer sets the speed of a clock and starts it running. As he plays each note, the machine at that instant records how many clock pulses have elapsed since the start of the sequence, and how many during the time that the note was held down. It simultaneously remembers which note on the keyboard was pressed and with what velocity it was struck. (The second parameter, or, indeed, the first, could equally be derived from any voltage source.) The composer continues until he has recorded perhaps sixty notes. He then restarts the clock and turns a switch which tells the machine that the next notes he plays will be directed to the second envelope shaper. While recording each sequence, he can simultaneously hear the results of what he has previously recorded.

The machine may then be set to the edit mode. In this mode the sequence may be advanced at any speed, or step by step, so that each note may be modified or erased. A special feature allows time to be *reversed*. A control rather like the spooling knob on studio tape recorders allows one to go forwards or backwards at any speed. Unlike a tape recorder, however, there is no inertia in the system, so that one can quite easily "zero in" on a particular note.

SEQUENCER CONTROLS

Ten controls are provided to adjust the amplitude of the sequencer's output voltages, and a further ten supervise the actual operation.

1. *Range of layer 1 output voltage A*
    This control is a slow motion dial calibrated 0–100. If Voltage A were used to control the pitch of an oscillator, then this control could be used to define the musical

interval for each step of the output. At 25, for instance, a range of sixty-four quarter tones (covering about $2\frac{1}{2}$ octaves) will be available.

2. *Range of layer 1 output voltage B*
The range of the second parameter for each event may similarly be adjusted with this control.

3. *Range of layer 1 keying voltage*
This voltage, which is positive for the duration of each note in Layer 1, would normally be used to control the envelope shaper. It can also be used to assist in the synthesis of certain instrumental sounds. For this reason, a centre zero control is provided. This inverts the polarity of the voltage when it is counterclockwise.
4, 5, and 6 are controls identical to 1, 2 and 3, except that they apply to the second layer. Likewise 7, 8 and 9, which apply to the third layer.

10. *Range of 'key 4'*
A fourth kind of event may be recorded which is similar to the three layers, except that there are no parameter control voltages available with it—just the keying voltage. It is primarily intended to stop or reset the sequencer's clock, allowing one to produce a single finite sequence or a repeating pattern. If not used for this purpose it might be used in conjunction with a slew limiter and a voltage controlled amplifier to initiate a crescendo or a number of other things.
Note that all controls, 1–10, can be adjusted after the sequence is entered, without changing the basic data.

11. *Clock rate*
This slow motion dial is a centre zero control in a rather special sense. When it is less than halfway, the sequence runs backwards. It controls the clock rate over a range of $\pm1000:1$. That is to say, with the control near its centre position, the clock pulses occur at about 2 per second, allowing a total sequence length of over six minutes. In this case, however, the resolution in time of each event is only half a second. The control has a distinct dead space

around half-way, which prevents the clock from "drifting" during editing.

A voltage proportional to the absolute clock speed is available at the control patchboard, so that it can simultaneously control all time variant parameters—envelope shapers, slew limiters and even oscillator frequencies—as the clock rate is adjusted.

12. *Note distribution*
This control is a four way switch; it tells the machine which of the three layers is being recorded, so that on replay the voltages will appear at the appropriate output. The fourth position denotes "Key 4" as described above.

13. *Stop at each note*
When this toggle switch is down, the sequencer clock stops at the start of each note that it reproduces.

14. *Stop at end of note*
Similar to 13, except that the sequencer stops at a time corresponding to when the key was released as the note was recorded.

These switches operate in conjunction with the note distribution switch, in that they only stop at a note in the layer defined by the latter.

The purpose of 13 and 14 is to facilitate the editing of events after a tentative sequence has been entered.

15. *Erase note button*
While this button is pressed, any notes in the layer selected by the note distribution switch which start at the time shown by the clock display, will be erased.

16. *Clear memory button*
This is the "bulk erase" button.

17. *Reset button*
This button sets the clock to zero, and holds it there as long as it is pressed. It does not stop the clock, it simply restarts the sequences from the beginning.

---

* *Note:* In this section, "Note" is used for musical convenience, but, it must be remembered, can be used for any parameter which has been selected.

18. *Start button*

This button allows the clock counter to start or continue counting. It would be used continually during editing, to advance the sequence note by note.

19. *Stop button*

This button stops the clock from counting.

Note that 17, 18 and 19 are momentary action push-buttons, not switches. They roughly correspond to the controls on a stop-watch.

When the sequencer clock is driven from pulses previously recorded on tape, or, indeed, from any external source, it will ignore them until the start button is pressed. Remote operation of the sequencer is facilitated by electrical inputs at the signal patchboard.

20. *Rewrite B, D, F*

When this switch is down, the second parameter voltages in each layer may be rewritten without disturbing the first parameter, or the event timing.

SUMMARY OF SPECIFICATION

Total storage capacity: 10,240 bits (of which 9216 bits are normally used).

ORGANISATION OF DATA:

36 bit words—each word representing one event.

Start-of-event time (referred to start of sequence)	10 bits
End-of-event time (referred to start of sequence)	10 bits
Selection of one of three envelope shapers and one pair (out of three pairs) of digital analog converters. Also internal functions	4 bits
Data, for digital analog converters	2 × 6 bits

DETAILS OF CODING

The 10 bit event time allows the start of each event to be defined to an accuracy of 1 part in 2 to the power 10 (viz. 1024).

Thus, if the clock is set to a rate of, say, one hundred pulses a second, each event may be adjusted forwards or backwards in increments of one hundredth of a second. The total sequence length would be ten seconds.

The "end of event" time, i.e., the time at which the key is released, is similarly recorded. Thus three control signals are reproduced, each being positive during the duration of a note intended for one of the three layers of the sequence. They are available at the patchboard as switching voltages which would normally go to the supervising inputs of the envelope shapers.

DIGITAL ANALOG CONVERTERS

Of the six converters, three are of accuracy appropriate to exact control of pitch on the diatonic scale. Six bits give a range of 64 notes. If greater range and/or finer resolution is required, then the output of the second converter may be added to that of the first. In this case, the player might use one keyboard to define a note on the diatonic scale, and the second to raise or lower that note by increments of one thirty-second of a tone.

The precise converters are accurate to $\pm 0\cdot 15\,\%$ (BSL). The second parameter converters are accurate to $\pm 0\cdot 7\,\%$ (BSL).

N   *Eight multifunction output amplifiers*

These amplifiers are primarily intended to be the last link in the signal chain before the tape recorder or monitor, but they provide certain subsidiary functions which will make them otherwise useful. All eight are voltage controlled ($0\cdot 5$ V per 6 dB).

CONTROLS

Level:	Slider type fader.
Pan:	A knob which distributes the output to between the left and right bus, these being common to four of the eight amplifiers.
Filter:	A single knob providing continuous transition between first order low pass and first order high pass.

Off switch: Totally disconnects output from the pan
                     control, allowing the amplifier to be used
                     earlier in the signal chain.
Meter switch: The meter may be used as a centre zero d.c.
                     voltmeter, or as an a.c. level meter.

O   *Two X–Y joystick controllers*

These give continuous control of two parameters together,
which is very useful in live performance. The control sticks
have a range of $2 \times \pm 2$ VDC.

P   *Two five-octave dynamically proportional keyboards*

Five octave keyboards giving precise divisions of pitch or any
other controllable parameter. In the case of pitch, the range
would give anything between 4 and 40 notes per octave. This is
useful for microtonal work. By setting 12 notes per octave, the
keyboard can be used as a normal melodic source.

A second voltage output is proportional to touch—actually
the velocity with which a key is struck. A third voltage switches
positive when one or more keys are pressed.

Note that the keyboard produces only one pitch voltage at
any instant; when several notes are pressed, the voltage of the
highest appears.

Both the pitch voltage and dynamic voltage are
"remembered," even when a key is released.

Keyboard voltage: 0·5 V per octave maximum, accurate to
                     better than 0·15 % at all points.
Dynamic voltage: $\pm 1·5$ V depending on key velocity.

Output function was synthesized to be a compromise between
a strict proportionality to velocity over a range of about 100:1,
and a function that would distribute seven subjectively equal
increments of playing force evenly over the output voltage
range. The keyboard feels most natural when the dynamics
voltage is used to control a modulator over a 40 dB range.

Q   *Eight-way fading/panning console* (See multifunction output
amplifiers)

R   *60 × 60 pin matrix patchboards* (7200 Pin Locations)

These patchboards allow any input to be connected to any output by the insertion of a single cordless pin. Each output is connected to a row of sixty horizontal holes. The holes appear as a square array of 3600 (×2) cross-points, in any of which a jack may be inserted. The jacks contain resistors so that several outputs may be mixed into a single input. All device outputs are fed to the board at a low impedance, blocking any reverse signal paths.

Two patchboards are provided, one intended for control signals and one for audio signals. A small number of inter-connection patches between the patchboards are hardwired, as some signals can be used in both domains.

It is also possible to route external signals to the patchboards by using the jacks in the conventional way. All contacts, including the jacks, have a surface coating of silver.

S   *Eight a.c./d.c. input amplifiers*

Maximum distortion at rated inputs: 0·1 %
Input sensitivities: line input: maximum 1·8 Va.c.
                                       (rms) or ±2·5 Vd.c.

These amplifiers convert input signals to a suitable level and impedance to feed treatment devices. The line inputs are directly coupled, and are therefore suitable for both signal and low frequency or d.c. control inputs. Two separate microphones amplifiers are supplied, which can feed any two of the above channels.

T   *Four external treatment send and returns*

Provision for sending out to external echo plates and other equipment, and returning to the Studio.

U   *One frequency to voltage converter*

This device accepts inputs from a variety of sources, including acoustical instruments (via a microphone or pickup and pre-amplifier) and produces a voltage proportional to the fundamental pitch of the note played. Sophisticated analog circuitry is incorporated to remove overtones, provided that their energy constitutes no more than 90 % of the total signal.

Unlike conventional frequency measuring techniques, which count the number of zero crossings of a waveform in a fixed interval of time, the converter measures the *period* of the signal and transforms this data to a voltage which is compatible with the other devices in the studio. The advantage of this method is that an accurate measure of the pitch can be made in a much shorter time. The output is gated into a track and hold buffer by a discriminator, which suppresses spurious outputs when the signal is dying away.

A single output control adjusts the range and polarity of the output voltage.

V   *Two envelope followers*

These devices produce a voltage proportional to the mean level of an audio signal. The output is passed through a second order low pass filter to remove ripple while keeping a fast response. Cut off is about 50 Hz.

Output amplitude is adjustable by a centre zero knob to give positive or negative excursions of up to 1 volt per 6 dB.

W   *Dawe 3000 AR/6 digital frequency meter*

Brief details as follows:

Crystal frequency:	100 KHz $\pm$ 0·002%
Frequency measurement:	Range: 0–1 MHz
	Accuracy: 1 digit $\pm$ crystal accuracy
	Gating time: 1 ms to 10 seconds
Period measurement:	Range: 0–300 KHz
	Time units 1 10 s to 10 ms
	Gating period: 1 to 1000 cycles of input frequency
Time measurement:	Range: 10 s–10^7 secs (nearly four months)

X   *Telequipment double beam oscilloscope, D43R*

Rack mounted double gun laboratory oscilloscope, with 6 × 8 cm display area.

Appendix 2

MUSYS Documentation standards

A programme written in the MUSYS Programming Language should always be fully documented: without documentation a programme listing or paper tape is virtually useless and might as well be thrown away. Where possible, the documentation should be "built in"—for example, programme and ASCII data listings may contain comments, and sufficiently detailed comments may even make other documentation a mere formality.

The documentation should start with a general description of the piece, and any special facilities or techniques required to realize it in the studio. A programme may have associated with it up to four paper tapes, and each of these should be accompanied by a listing:

1 A *source tape* of the MUSYS Programme.
2 A *data tape* (*ASCII Format*) containing extra data to be read during compilation.
3 A *binary tape* containing the compiled data in compact form (this tape may be loaded directly without compiling, and therefore provides the most rapid way of performing a piece. Its length may make a full listing impracticable, but if a full listing is required, it can be achieved with the "W" command).

4 A *Table Data Tape* will be required if the MUSYS 64-word tables have to be edited before the piece is played. If the alterations to the standard tables are very simple, editing instructions can be included, but it is safer and simpler to dump the whole field containing the tables and reload it prior to performance.

In addition to these tapes and listings, the following information is necessary.

5 A list of the MUSYS devices used.

6 The patch required. There are several ways of describing the patch: possibilities are a list of the interconnections required, a block diagram of the devices used and their connections, or a diagram of the patch panel itself on squared paper with the pins marked as blobs.

7 Manual control settings for Line Amplifiers, Mixers, etc.

8 Settings and instructions for any extra devices used, such as the VCS-4, extra tape decks, external inputs.

9 The optimum performance speed, unless this is delivered directly to the clock by the program.

10 If a piece requires multi-tracking, the format of the tape used for recording it should be explained fully.

Part of a composition, programmed on the Synthi – 100

"AN EXAMPLE OF A MUSYS III PROGRAMME"

"HAYDN: SONATA XXXIV"

"THE FINAL VERSION IS ON 3 TRACKS EACH BEING VARIANTS OF THE SAME PROGRAMME. THIS IS FOR TRACK 1."
"THIS PROGRAMME PLAYS THE FIRST PART OF THE FINALE TWISTING AROUND VARIOUS PARAMETERS TO MAKE VARIATIONS ON THE EXACT DATA PROVIDED BY PAPER TAPE. THE PROGRAMME MAKES SOME USE OF ALL THE USUAL MUSYS III COMPILER FACILITIES. THIS EXAMPLE HAS LAVISH COMMENTS."

"PATCH: O1-E1, O2-E2, O3-E3. E1+E2−A4, E3−A5.
A4−F2, A5−F3. F2−MA1, F3−MA2. A4−MA3, A5−MA4. MA-OUT."

"INITIALISATION"
1! W1.0. T1.60. W1.1. U1.0. "MELODY VOICE ON BUS 3, REST ON BUS 1"
2! W2.0. T1.60. W2.1.
3! W3.0. #FLT2 1; #FLT3 1; T1.60. W3.1.

"MAIN PERFORMANCE PROGRAMME"

"#SM AND #SA (MELODY AND ACCOMPANIMENT) REQUIRE 6 PARAMETERS"
"NOTE VALUE, TIME VALUE, ATTACK, DECAY, LOUDNESS AND FILTERING LIST NUMBER"
"#SM ALSO SPECIFIES THE SEVENTH PARAMETER OF INTER-RUPT RATE"
COMMENTS FOR EACH VARIATION DO NOT INDICATE EACH PARAMETER CHANGE."

"MAIN THEME PLAYS IT MECHANICALLY STRAIGHT"
#SM ←, ←, 5, 3, 15, 1 8; #SA ←, ←, 5, 3, 15, 1;
"VARIATION 1: RANDOM NOTES IN ACCOMPANIMENT"
#SM ← −42, ←, 6, 3, 15, 2, 6; #SA ←*φ 63 ↑, ←, 6, 7, 14, 2;
"VARIATION 2: MOVES BASS UP TREBLE DOWN"
#SM #ZE −24;, ←, 5, 3, 15, 3, 8; #SA #ZE 24;, ←, 5, 3, 14, 3;
"VARIATION 3: POSITIONED RANDOM NOTES IN BOTH CLEFS"
#SM #ZE −6 ↑ + 6;, ←, 6, 2, 14, 4, 7; #SA ← −14 ↑, ←, 6, 2, 14, 4;
"VARIATION 4: STRAIGHT WITH WOODWIND FILTERING"
#SM ←, ←, 5, 3, 14, 5, 8; #SA ←, ←, 5, 3, 14, 5;

Bibliography

H. Badings and J. W. de Bruyn, *Philips Technical Review*, Vol 19 No 6, 1957

Milton Babbit, "The Synthesis, Perception and Specification of Musical Time," *International Folk Music*, Vol 16, 1964

Milton Babbit, "*The Use of Computers in Musicological Research*, Princeton University Press, Princeton, N.J., 1965

Herbert Brun, "Technology and the Composer," *UNESCO Conference on Music and Technology, Stockholm, June 1970*

Gustav Ciamaga, "Training of the Composer in New Technological Means," *UNESCO Conference on Music and Technology, Stockholm, June 1970*

Gustav Ciamaga and J. Gabura, University of Toronto, Canada

A. Douglas, *Electrical Production of Music*, Philosophical Library, New York, 1957.

Electronic Music Studios (London) Ltd, *A Summary of MUSYS Commands*, Vol 6

Electronic Music Studios (London) Ltd, *An Electronic Music Language and System Developed in London*

F. Enkel, *Tech Hausmitt NWDR*, Vol 6, Nos 42–46, 1954

A. Forte, "A Programme for Analytic Reading of Scores," *J. Music Theory*, No 10, 1966

G. Gurvitch, "Les Variations des Perceptions Collectives des Entendues," *Cahiers Internationaux de Soliologie*, Vol 37, 1964

L. A. Hiller and R. A. Baker, "Automated Music Printing," *J. Music Theory*, No 9, 1865

L. A. Hiller and L. M. Isaacson, *Experimental Music*, McGraw-Hill Book Co, New York

H. Jacobi and A. Schmidt, "Reaktanzvierpole als Filter," *V.N.*, Vol 2, 1932

J. Audio Eng Soc, New York

Werner Kaegi, "Music and Technology in the Europe of 1970," *UNESCO Conference on Music and Technology, Stockholm, June 1970*

Werner Kaegi, *Was ist elektronische Musik*, Zurich, 1967

G. M. Koenig, "The Use of Computer Programmes in Creating Music," *UNESCO Conference on Music and Technology, Stockholm, June 1970*

Lewis and MacLaren, *J. Soc. Motion Picture Eng*, Vol 50, No 3

Max Matthews, "Electronic Sound Studio of the 1970's," *UNESCO Conference on Music and Technology, Stockholm, June 1970*

Max Matthews, *Music by Computers*, Cambridge, Mass

Matthews, Pierce and Gutman, *Gravsaner Blatter*, No 23, 1962

W. Meyer-Eppler, *Elektronische Musik*, Berlin, 1955.

W. Meyer-Eppler, "Elektronisches Kompositions Technik," *Melos*, Vol 20, 1953

Abraham Moles, "Informationstheorie der Musik," *Nachtenrichtentechnische Fachberichte*, Vol 3, Braunschweig, 1946

Robert A. Moog, "A Voltage Controlled Lowpass Highpass Filter for Audio Signal Processing," *J. Audio Eng Soc*, 1965

Robert A. Moog, "Voltage Controlled Electronic Modules," *J. Audio Eng Soc*, Vol 13, No 3, 1965

Music, Physics and Engineering, Dover Publishing Inc, New York

H. F. Olson and H. Belar, *J. Acoustical Soc America*, Vol 33, No 9

R. C. Pinkerton, *Scientific American*, Vol 194, No 2, 1956

J. C. Risset, *An Introductory Catalogue of Computer Sounds*, Bell Telephone Laboratories, Murray Hill, N.J.

O. Sala, "Experimentalle Grundlagen des Trautoniums," *Frequenz*, Vol 2, 1932

Pierre Schaeffer, "La Musique et les Ordinateurs," *UNESCO Conference on Music and Technology, Stockholm, June 1970*

C. A. Seashore, *Psychology of Music*, Dover Publishing, New York; Constable, London, 1968

Shannon and Weaver, *Mathematical Theory of Communication*, University of Illinois Press, Urbana, 1949

Minao Shibata, "Music and Technology in Japan," *UNESCO Conference on Music and Technology, Stockholm, June 1970*

F. Trautwein, *Elektronische Musik*, Verlag Weidmann, Berlin, 1930

F. Trautwein, "Toneinsatz und electronische Musik," *Z. Tech Phys*, No 13, 1932

V. A. Ussachevsky, *J. Audio Eng Soc New York*, Vol 6, No 3

F. Winckel, "Electronische Steurung multivariabler Räume," *Buhnentechnische Rundschau*, No 2, 1967

I. Xenaxia, "Musique Formelles," *La Revue Musicale*, 253, Paris, 1968

P. Zinovieff, *A Computerized Music Studio*, Electronic Music Report, Inst of Sonology, Utrecht State University, 1969

P. Zinovieff, "The Special Case of Inspirational Computer Music Scores,' *London Magazine*, July 1969

Index